CSR, Sustainability, Ethics & Governance

In recent years the discussion concerning the relation between business and society has made immense strides. This has in turn led to a broad academic and practical discussion on innovative management concepts, such as Corporate Social Responsibility, Corporate Governance and Sustainability Management. This series offers a comprehensive overview of the latest theoretical and empirical research and provides sound concepts for sustainable business strategies. In order to do so, it combines the insights of leading researchers and thinkers in the fields of management theory and the social sciences – and from all over the world, thus contributing to the interdisciplinary and intercultural discussion on the role of business in society. The underlying intention of this series is to help solve the world's most challenging problems by developing new management concepts that create value for business and society alike. In order to support those managers, researchers and students who are pursuing sustainable business approaches for our common future, the series offers them access to cutting-edge management approaches.

CSR, Sustainability, Ethics & Governance is accepted by the Norwegian Register for Scientific Journals, Series and Publishers, maintained and operated by the Norwegian Social Science Data Services (NSD)

More information about this series at http://www.springer.com/series/11565

Manuel Castelo Branco

Corporate Social Responsibility, the Fight Against Corruption and Tax Behaviour

Springer

Manuel Castelo Branco
School of Economics and Management
University of Porto
Porto, Portugal

ISSN 2196-7075 ISSN 2196-7083 (electronic)
CSR, Sustainability, Ethics & Governance
ISBN 978-3-662-63733-3 ISBN 978-3-662-63735-7 (eBook)
https://doi.org/10.1007/978-3-662-63735-7

This Springer imprint is published by the registered company Springer-Verlag GmbH, DE part of Springer Nature.
The registered company address is: Heidelberger Platz 3, 14197 Berlin, Germany

Preface

Corruption and associated phenomena and certain types of corporate tax behaviour (such as tax avoidance) are persistent problems of capitalism. In more recent decades, they have spurred continuing attention. They have become highly scrutinized issues, as evidenced by the creation and development of civil society organizations such as the Transparency International or the Tax Transparency Network. Notwithstanding, only relatively recently the fight against corruption and responsible tax behaviour have become well-established aspects of corporate social responsibility (CSR).

This book intends to provide students and scholars interested in CSR and in how corporations can contribute to sustainable development with a succinct analysis of these two relatively neglected CSR issues. The arguments put forward in this book build on previous theoretical developments in a number of academic fields, such as economics, ethics, law, or management. Such developments include, but are not limited to, theoretical developments related to Amartya Sen's approach to development, Paul Ricoeur's understanding of ethics, Cécile Renouard's approach to business ethics and CSR, Eric Chaffee's collaboration theory of the corporation, and Avi Yonah's views on corporate taxation and CSR. The approaches to the economy, ethics, development, the corporation, and CSR developed by these researchers, among others, have been instrumental in the development of my views on the fight against corruption and responsible tax behaviour as CSR issues.

My engagement with these issues dates at least from the beginning of the decade that has just ended. Such engagement occurred in great part due to my involvement with the OBEGEF—*Observatório de Economia e Gestão de Fraude* (Observatory in Economics and Management of Fraud), a couple of years after its creation in 2008 as a non-profit private law association. It has as its host institution the University of Porto, in Portugal, more specifically its School of Economics and Management, where it has its headquarters. I owe a debt of gratitude to Professor Carlos Pimenta, founder and former director of the OBEGEF. He is responsible for my interest in the topic of corruption. Because of my involvement with this organization, I have been able to attend some conferences at which the issues examined in this book featured prominently, to have discussions on them at several venues, as well as publish some articles and working papers on them. I thank the School of Economics and Management of the University of Porto for providing me an academic home during the past two decades, in which I was able to develop my teaching and research activities. *A thanks is also due to the* editorial team at Springer Nature for their assistance in preparing this book.

A final thanks must go to my lovely wife and frequent coauthor, Catarina Delgado. Besides supporting and encouraging me throughout the period of working on this project, she was a source of valuable criticism, comments, ideas, and suggestions during the entire writing process of this book.

Porto, Portugal Manuel Castelo Branco

Contents

Abbreviations

CPI	Corruption Perceptions Index
CSR	Corporate Social Responsibility
EITI	Extractive Industries Transparency Initiative
EU	European Union
EU NFRD	European Union Non-Financial Reporting Directive
FDI	Foreign Direct Investment
GDP	Gross Domestic Product
GRI	Global Reporting Initiative
HM	Her Majesty
IMF	International Monetary Fund
ISO	International Organization for Standardization
MNEs	Multinational Enterprises
NFR	Non-Financial Reporting
OECD	Organization for Economic Co-operation and Development
PRI	Principles for Responsible Investment
SDGs	Sustainable Development Goals
SEC	Securities and Exchange Commission
TI	Transparency International
TRAC	Transparency in Corporate Reporting
UK	United Kingdom
UNCTAD	United Nations Conference on Trade and Development
UNGC	United Nations Global Compact
US	United States of America
USAID	United States Agency for International Development

List of Figures

List of Tables

Chapter 1
Introduction

Abstract This is an introductory chapter in which the concept of corporate social responsibility (CSR) is introduced and the fight against corruption and responsible tax behaviour are presented as CSR issues. The present-day importance of corruption and taxation for citizens explaining why the two issues under examination came to the fore is also discussed. The view of the corporation and its role in modern societies upheld in this book is succinctly presented and the implications of such a view for the conceptualizations of corporate practices such as the ones explored here are briefly discussed. The purposes of the book and its structure are presented.

Keywords Corporate social responsibility · Fight against corruption · Responsible tax behaviour

1.1 Background

One way of looking at corporate social responsibility (CSR) is to view it as "the responsibility of enterprises for their impact on society" (European Commission, 2011, p. 6). This definition was offered by the European Commission in a document published in 2011, which reported on the EU's CSR policy for the period 2011–14. It is a fairly simple definition that can be adopted as a starting point for this book.

Corruption, tax evasion, and tax avoidance are so widely known phenomena, they are so present in the media that I believe defining them in the introduction to this book is dispensable. Fighting corruption and responsible tax behaviour[1] are some of the issues associated with CSR whose relative importance has increased the most in

[1]Some researchers offer interesting discussions regarding the terminology one should (or should not) use when discussing tax behaviour in articulation with CSR (Hasseldine & Morris, 2018; Oats & Tuck, 2019). Albeit acknowledging their value and the validity of the arguments presented by these researchers, I will not enter such discussions in this book in view of its introductory character. Hence, I will utilize the term "responsible" when referring to tax behaviour (practices, strategies, conduct, etc.), given that it is widely used in the literature, by "activists" (Boerrild et al., 2015; Fair

M. Castelo Branco, *Corporate Social Responsibility, the Fight Against Corruption and Tax Behaviour*, CSR, Sustainability, Ethics & Governance,
https://doi.org/10.1007/978-3-662-63735-7_1

recent years. Although the fight against corruption is today a well-established CSR topic, the case was not always the same, even in our century. Just about 9 years ago, Hess (2012, p. 45) could assert that, in the earlier years of our century, it "was excluded from many major CSR initiatives, but in the last few years it has become a central topic". About 8 years ago, KPMG (2013) considered these two issues as constituting, at the time, a kind of new wave of CSR.

Regarding tax behaviour, in the late 2000s, Susan Symons and some PricewaterhouseCoopers colleagues devoted their attention to CSR and corporate tax behaviour (Landolf & Symons, 2008; Scheiwiller & Symons, 2010). Landolf and Symons (2008) acknowledge that relative to social and environmental issues, the economic dimension of corporate responsibility was, at the time, the least developed, and it was more often than not equated to financial performance. Two years later, Scheiwiller and Symons (2010, p. 28) stated their belief that "paying tax has already started to develop as a corporate responsibility issue". These professionals started their argument using the case of workers' health and safety as an example of a well-established CSR issue that 20 years earlier was in the first stages of its development as such. Their expectation seemed to be that a similar process was occurring with tax behaviour. Five years later, a researcher at the International Centre for Tax and Development asked whether responsible tax behaviour would be the next frontier of CSR (McCluskey, 2015).

Meanwhile, the importance of these topics as CSR-related issues has increased immensely. In a very recent book on the "main challenges in managing sustainable business" (Arvidsson, 2019), two of its five parts are devoted to "anti-corruption and business ethics" (Part IV) and "Ethical Taxation and Tax Transparency" (Part V) (the other parts being on sustainability reporting, sustainability assurance, and sustainable finance).

One could label the fight against corruption and responsible tax behaviour as emerging issues of CSR because only relatively recently they have risen to prominence within CSR instruments, such as the Global Reporting Initiative (GRI) Standards for sustainability reporting and the United Nations Global Compact (UNGC). An additional reason to label them as such pertains to the fact that only in recent times they have become well-established topics of academic research, as evidenced by only very recently having been published the first literature reviews on these topics.

In the case of the fight against corruption, it was not considered in the first versions of the two CSR instruments mentioned above, being added only in later versions. An important milestone in its rise to prominence was the inclusion of corruption-related indicators in the second version of the GRI sustainability reporting guidelines (GRI, 2002). In more recent versions of these guidelines, its importance has increased, and the number of indicators on this issue reached as much as five (GRI, 2013). When the GRI Standards were published in 2016, a

Tax Mark, 2020), practitioners (Landolf & Symons, 2008), and researchers (Bird & Davis-Nozemack, 2018; Hardeck & Hertl, 2014; Muller & Kolk, 2015; Scarpa & Signori, 2020).

specific standard was proposed on the subject (GRI 205: Anti-corruption 2016). Also important was the addition, in 2004, to the set of principles initially proposed by the UNGC in 2001 (related to human rights, labour, and environment), of an additional principle (the 10th) specifically devoted to the fight against corruption. In the case of responsible tax behaviour, its rise is much more recent. This issue only deserved a specific standard under the GRI Standards in 2019 (GRI 207: Tax 2019) (GRI, 2020).

Interestingly enough, the World Economic Forum's (in collaboration with Deloitte, EY, KPMG, and PwC) recent attempt at providing a set of metrics and disclosures pertaining to CSR policies and practices includes proposed metrics and disclosures concerning these two issues (WEF, 2020). WEF (2020) organises the metrics and disclosures it proposes into the following four pillars: Principles of Governance, People, Planet, and Prosperity. The issue of the fight against corruption is considered under the theme "ethical behaviour", which is part of the Governance pillar. The issue of responsible tax behaviour is considered under the themes "employment and wealth generation" and "community and social vitality", which are part of the Prosperity pillar.

Concerning the topics under consideration, as far as I am aware, only very recently (in the last 3 years) the first reviews of literature were published in reputable scientific journals or as book chapters (Bahoo, 2020; Bahoo et al., 2020; Moisé, 2020; Scarpa & Signori, 2020; Whait et al., 2018). In 2018 the first literature review on the relationship between CSR and tax behaviour was published (Whait et al., 2018). Only in 2020 were published the first literature reviews on corruption in international business (Bahoo et al., 2020) and in specific sectors, such as in banks (Bahoo, 2020) and in the oil sector (Moisé, 2020). Rygh (2021, p. 86) establishes the relationship between these issues, stating that "supporting tax havens may also indirectly contribute to corruption and money laundering". Rygh refers to tax evasion and tax avoidance as emerging CSR issues.

Among the reasons for such an increase in importance of corruption and taxation is the fact that such issues are amidst those that have a greater influence on the trust that citizens have in corporations and governments. Clear evidence of this is the answers to the question "what can businesses do that would cause the most damage to your trust in a better future?" which was included in the survey used in the data collection for the 2017 Edelman Trust Barometer – Global Report (Edelman, 2017). The three actions of corporations that the respondents considered to be most damaging to such trust were, in order of importance, the payment of bribes to government officials to obtain contracts, the payment to executives of amounts much higher than those paid to other employees, and the transfer of profits to other countries for the purpose of reducing the tax burden. Corruption, tax avoidance, and tax evasion are, then, among the phenomena that concern citizens the most.

These issues are increasingly not only at the basis of voluntary business practices, usually included in the scope of what is understood as CSR, but are also increasingly subject to regulation by governments. In both cases, the aim is undoubtedly to reduce the gap between what citizens expect from corporations and their actual practices.

I should also note that corruption and tax behaviour are inextricably related to economic inequality, which is the other area of concern identified by citizens worldwide. Inequality can be considered as something that arises, directly or indirectly, in a linear or complex manner, from irresponsible practices by corporations in terms of tax behaviour and corruption and related phenomena. Moreover, several of the difficulties currently experienced in implementing policies to address many of the environmental problems we face, particularly those pertaining to climate change, are related to fraud, corruption, and related phenomena such as lobbying. This relationship with inequality, among other consequences they have, is one of the reasons explaining why corruption and tax behaviour are inextricably linked to sustainable development.

Business practices can have an indirect influence on inequality, for example, through tax evasion and fraud or lobbying for regulations that are beneficial to business but harmful to society (Bapuji et al., 2020, p. 1208). Such practices can also exert their influence "in a complex manner (e.g., corporate social responsibility [CSR] aimed at community development or promoting shareholder wealth maximisation as a firm's primary mandate)" (ibid.). Lobbying for regulations that are beneficial to business but harmful to society is also a factor that has proven extremely damaging to the creation of the necessary legislation to properly address environmental problems.

The view of the corporation's role upheld in this book apprehends it as a primary institution of capitalism, and more broadly of our societies, as is also the case with the market or the state (Chassagnon, 2012). Hence, in responding to Dallas's (1988, p. 19) question of whether corporations are "mere commodities that can be bought and sold, or are they political and social institutions that must be handled in a different way", I take the latter view. The social role of the corporation is viewed here as that of obtaining and using a number of diverse resources (those that it owns, but also public and common resources) with a view of producing and distributing the goods and/or services intended to satisfy individual or collective needs, generating the revenues necessary for its members to continue to engage with it in a way that the corporation can continue to perform such a role. This obviously includes the profit necessary for its survival but is surely not limited to it. The corporation is viewed as a collaboration between a number of individuals and entities, including governments, which often have conflicting interests.

Corporations' activities have a positive social impact, but they also produce deleterious consequences to society. According to Mayer (2013, p. 23), "at the same time as it is feeding, housing, educating, and transporting us", the corporation "is also exploiting, polluting, poisoning, and impoverishing us". Concerning this latter aspect, Mayer recalls the numerous environmental disasters (e.g. those in Bhopal, Love Canal, and the Gulf of Mexico) and the countless financial disasters (e.g. those associated with Barings, Enron and World-Com) and accounting scandals (such as Xerox or Satyam) (ibid.).

In view of the conceptualisation of the corporation and its role presented above, I suggest that when a corporation knowingly exploits and impoverish us, as well as when it pollutes and poison us and the natural environment in which we live, the corporation has been corrupted in the sense that it does not work in a manner that is consistent with its role and the function which is supposed to play. This perspective is consistent with Fleming and Zyglidopoulos's (2009) idea that corporate corruption can be expanded to include activities considered as corporate crime, such as anti-competitive behaviour, illegal environmental damage, irresponsible working conditions, marketing and sale of unsafe products, or tax evasion. This idea stems from a view of corporate corruption as encompassing not only situations in which the individuals in the organisation benefit but also situations that aim at and result in benefits for the whole organisation rather than specific individuals in it (ibid.).

I suggest that Fleming and Zyglidopoulos's (2009) expanded definition of corruption can be further expanded to also include activities that do not conform to the definition of corporate crime. This is the case of corporate activities that are beneficial (actually or potentially) to the corporation while being detrimental to society as a whole, such as lobbying or the funding of political parties.

I am convinced that these perspectives are not fundamentally different from the one underpinning the recent Transparency International UK's proposal of guidance on corporate anti-corruption reporting (Transparency International UK, 2020). This organisation's approach has been that of identifying five key areas considered of a high risk of corporate corruption and providing guidance on disclosure pertaining to them. Besides reporting on anti-corruption programmes, Transparency International UK considers fundamental the reporting on:

- "The natural person who directly or indirectly ultimately owns or controls" the corporation (p.30) (beneficial ownership reporting).
- "Fully consolidated subsidiaries and non-fully consolidated holdings" (p. 34) (organisational structure reporting).
- Financial data for countries in which the corporation operates, including payments to governments (country-by-country reporting).
- Engagement in political activities, such as political contributions, lobbying, and the phenomenon of individuals moving "in either direction, between positions in the public and private sectors" (p. 46), usually called "revolving door" (corporate political engagement reporting).

1.2 Scope and Aims

This is a book on the role of corporations both in engaging in corruption and in combating it, both in engaging in tax evasion and tax avoidance and in contributing their fair share. Hence, it is a book both on corporate social irresponsibility and on corporate social responsibility. It addresses a broad range of phenomena that may be inextricably linked to the two issues under examination, ranging from corporate lobbying to corporate political connections. For example, the phenomenon of corruption cannot be understood adequately without addressing these latter phenomena. This means that we will also deal with what has come to be called "corruption,

American style" (Stiglitz, 2016) and with what some call the supply side of corruption (Palan et al., 2010).

The aim of this book is to introduce in an accessible way how CSR and the reporting thereof are being used to address the problems of corruption and tax evasion and tax avoidance. It seeks to offer a presentation and discussion of the efforts, both of organisations and governments, to integrate these issues into CSR practices and the developments that have occurred at the level of legislation, national, and international, through which governments compel or try to induce companies to have practices more in line with what is expected of them in terms of combating corruption and paying their fair share. In particular, CSR voluntary instruments, such as the UNGC, the Organisation for Economic Co-operation and Development (OECD) Guidelines for Multinational Enterprises (MNEs), the GRI's standards for sustainability reporting, or the ISO 26000 will be addressed. Multi-stakeholder initiatives such as the Extractive Industries Transparency Initiative (EITI) will also be considered in the analysis. Recent developments in corporate reporting legislation, such as non-financial reporting and country-by-country reporting, which have recently become mandatory for certain types of corporations in the European Union, will also be considered.

The purposes of the book are related to what has just been described. First, it tries to present a set of socio-economic changes that occurred in recent decades that have brought to the fore the topics discussed here and led to their inclusion in the list of priorities of many organisations, including governments and companies. Second, it intends to discuss how the issues under analysis have come to be prominent issues in public policy and in CSR-related policies. Third, it purports to present how the main instruments related to CSR address the issues on which this book focuses. Finally, it aims to highlight the role of the requirement for greater transparency, in particular through stricter disclosure requirements, in the efforts made by public authorities to regulate and contribute to the mitigation of the problems associated with such issues.

Primarily intended for a wide array of audiences, including undergraduate and graduate students of CSR and business ethics, practitioners, researchers on CSR and corruption issues, and the general public interested in corruption, tax, and CSR issues, parts of this book will probably seem simplistic for some and completely new for others.

1.3 Structure

The book is divided into two parts. The first part is devoted to a presentation of what is at stake in CSR. It can be considered introductory in that it sets the stage for the subsequent discussion of the issues on which this book focuses. Underlying any perspective on CSR is a certain view of the economy, ethics, development, and the relationship between them. A certain view of the corporation and its role in the economy also underpins such a perspective. This is so because, as Colombo (2017, p. 821) so neatly puts it, the modern corporation "overflows with interpersonal interactions, and continuously implicates how we, as human beings, ought to treat one another". This researcher adds that corporate law could be depicted in the same way. I would add that the same is the case with the modern economy. I am convinced that such underlying views should be made explicit before developing any CSR-related concepts. This will be done in chapters two and three in the most synthetic and straightforward manner I am capable of. The fourth chapter is devoted to the presentation of CSR and its main instruments.

The second part is devoted to the specific CSR-related issues on which this book focuses. It is composed of two chapters, one for each of the issues under examination: the fight against corruption and tax behaviour. I suggest that corporations are both a major part of the problem and of the solution. A special focus is laid on the international endeavours to improve transparency through corporate reporting, and the two chapters elaborate on the UNGC, the OECD Guidelines for MNEs, the GRI Standards, and the so-called European Union Non-Financial Reporting Directive (EU NFRD). These initiatives are considered to play an important role in providing the trust-based informal social norms, without which markets and societies cannot function. Other relevant initiatives will also be addressed, albeit more briefly.

These two chapters present a similar structure. Corporate corruption and irresponsible tax behaviour are defined, and their causes and consequences on society are analysed. Both issues are depicted as incompatible with sustainable development, given the social, economic, and environmental damages caused by them. The fight against corruption and responsible tax behaviour are analysed as CSR issues and are presented as integral parts of any corporation's social responsibility. CSR-related instruments are presented, and the issue of how these instruments may help is discussed. The book outlines the importance of anti-corruption and responsible tax CSR policies and the reporting thereof as a basis for an effective fight against these problems.

Chapter five explores the role of CSR in the fight against corruption. In this chapter, discussions on corruption and its effects, as well as on how the CSR-related instruments mentioned above may help in such a fight, are offered. In chapter six, the relation between the tax behaviour of corporations and CSR is explored. The negative consequences of corporate tax avoidance and evasion are highlighted, namely those affecting nations. The argument that the pernicious social consequences of the generalised use of tax minimisation strategies by corporations make their tax behaviour a matter of business assumption of social responsibilities is presented. Moreover, I put forward the argument that whatever the view of the corporation one upholds, strategies conceived by corporations with the sole purpose of minimising their tax burden are considered to be incoherent with the notion of CSR. The book concludes with some final remarks.

References

Arvidsson, S. (2019). *Challenges in managing sustainable business*. Palgrave Macmillan.

Bahoo, S. (2020). Corruption in banks: A bibliometric review and agenda. *Finance Research Letters, 35*, 101499.

Bahoo, S., Alon, I., & Paltrinieri, A. (2020). Corruption in international business: A review and research agenda. *International Business Review, 29*(4), 101660.

Bapuji, H., Patel, C., Ertug, G., & Allen, D. G. (2020). Corona crisis and inequality: Why management research needs a societal turn. *Journal of Management, 46*(7), 1205–1222.

Bird, R., & Davis-Nozemack, K. (2018). Tax avoidance as a sustainability problem. *Journal of Business Ethics, 151*(4), 1009–1025.

Boerrild, T., Kohonen, M., Sarin, R., Stares, K., & Lewis, M. (2015). *Getting to good: Towards responsible corporate tax behaviour*. Oxfam.

Chassagnon, V. (2012). Nature et ontologie sociale de la firme. *Social Science Information, 51*(1), 70–95.

Colombo, R. J. (2017). Religious conceptions of corporate purpose. *Washington and Lee Law Review, 74*(2), 813–845.

Dallas, L. L. (1988). Two models of corporate governance: Beyond Berle and means. *University of Michigan Journal of Law Reform, 22*(1), 19–116.

Edelman. (2017). *2017 Edelman trust barometer - global report*. Edelman.

European Commission (2011). *Communication from the commission to the European parliament, the Council, the European economic and social committee and the committee of the regions*. A renewed EU strategy 2011–14 for Corporate Social Responsibility. COM 2011(681) final.

Fair Tax Mark. (2020). *The essential elements of global corporate standards for responsible tax conduct (public consultation draft)*. Fair Tax Mark.

Fleming, P., & Zyglidopoulos, S. C. (2009). *Charting corporate corruption: Agency*. Edward Elgar Publishing.

GRI. (2002). *Sustainability reporting guidelines*. GRI.

GRI. (2013). *Sustainability reporting guidelines – G4*. GRI.

GRI. (2020). *Consolidated set of GRI sustainability reporting standards 2020*. GRI.

Hardeck, I., & Hertl, R. (2014). Consumer reactions to corporate tax strategies: Effects on corporate reputation and purchasing behavior. *Journal of Business Ethics, 123*(2), 309–326.

Hasseldine, J., & Morris, G. (2018). Unacceptable tax behaviour and corporate responsibility. In N. Hashimzade & Y. Epifantseva (Eds.), *The Routledge companion to tax avoidance research* (pp. 430–457). Routledge.

Hess, D. (2012). Combating corruption through corporate transparency: Using enforcement discretion to improve disclosure. *Minnesota Journal of International Law, 21*, 42–70.

Landolf, U., & Symons, S. (2008). Applying corporate responsibility to tax. *International Tax Review, 44*, 6–13.

Mayer, C. (2013). *Firm commitment: Why the corporation is failing us and how to restore trust in it*. Oxford University Press.

McCluskey, R. (2015). *Is responsible tax behaviour the next frontier of CSR?* Accessed Oct 20, 2020, from https://www.ictd.ac/blog/is-responsible-tax-behaviour-the-next-frontier-of-csr/

Moisé, G. M. (2020). Corruption in the oil sector: A systematic review and critique of the literature. *The Extractive Industries and Society, 7*(1), 217–236.

Muller, A., & Kolk, A. (2015). Responsible tax as corporate social responsibility: The case of multinational enterprises and effective tax in India. *Business and Society, 54*(4), 435–463.

Oats, L., & Tuck, P. (2019). Corporate tax avoidance: Is tax transparency the solution? *Accounting and Business Research, 49*(5), 565–583.

Palan, R., Murphy, R., & Chavagneux, C. (2010). *Tax havens: How globalisation really works*. Cornell University Press.

Rygh, A. (2021). Multinational enterprises and economic inequality: A review and international business research agenda. *Critical Perspectives on International Business, 17*(1), 72–102.

Scarpa, F., & Signori, S. (2020). Ethics of corporate taxation: A systematic literature review. In J. D. Rendtorff (Ed.), *Handbook of business legitimacy* (pp. 459–485). Springer.

Scheiwiller, T., & Symons, S. (2010). Corporate responsibility and paying tax. *OECD Observer, 276*(277), 27–28.

Stiglitz, J. E. (2016). *The state, the market, and developmen*t. WIDER Working Paper No. 2016/1.

Transparency International UK. (2020). *Open business: Principles and guidance for anti-corruption corporate transparency*. Transparency International UK.

Whait, R. B., Christ, K. L., Ortas, E., & Burritt, R. L. (2018). What do we know about tax aggressiveness and corporate social responsibility? An integrative review. *Journal of Cleaner Production, 204*, 542–552.

World Economic Forum (WEF). (2020). *Measuring stakeholder capitalism–towards common metrics and consistent reporting of sustainable value creation*. WEF.

Part I
Contextualising Corporate Social Responsibility

Chapter 2
The Economy, Ethics, and Development

Abstract In this chapter the views of the economy, ethics, development, and the relationship between them that underpin the perspective on CSR upon which this book rests are presented. The chapter helps setting the stage for the subsequent discussion of the issues on which this book focuses. The concept of sustainable human development associated with the work of Amartya Sen is linked to CSR, which is depicted as the contribution of corporations to such development.

Keywords The economy · Ethics · Sustainable human development

2.1 The Economy

The perspective that underpins the approach to CSR adopted in this book is based on views that place man at the epicentre of the economy, as is the case of the ones proposed by researchers such as Karl William Kapp, Karl Polanyi, François Perroux, Amartya Sen, and Cécile Renouard.

The first issue one has to address is the view of the economy. In his "A New Concept of Development", François Perroux (2010), one of the great thinkers of economic development of the twentieth century defended that the development of each man and of all men is a goal that should be unanimously accepted by those responsible for politics, the economy, and research. This statement is based on a view of the economy that emphasises the relationships that are established between people and groups of people, apprehending the economy as the organisation, to the advantage of each and everyone, of human relationships through the use of goods that are scarce socially and approximately quantifiable and accountable for (Perroux, 2010).

Regarding Perroux's view of the economy, Maréchal (2003, p. 53) emphasises the following three aspects:

– Instead of focusing on the relations between human beings and wealth, this view highlights the relations between human beings.

M. Castelo Branco, *Corporate Social Responsibility, the Fight Against Corruption and Tax Behaviour*, CSR, Sustainability, Ethics & Governance,
https://doi.org/10.1007/978-3-662-63735-7_2

- The restriction of the relations to be studied to those that have to do with scarce goods leads to not recognising any pretension to the constitution of an all-encompassing understanding of human action.
- The emphasis on the social character of the quantification of scarce goods refers to the socially constructed dimension of scarcity.

Maréchal (2003, p. 62) also highlights the proximity between the thought of Perroux and Amartya Sen, explored below, albeit there is no evidence of Perroux having influenced Sen.

Perroux's view is consistent with a view of the economy, to which I adhere, that results from a re-reading of Aristotle with a focus on the analysis of the main problems that we face today. Such re-reading has been pursued by economists such as Crespo (2013a, b, 2017a, b, 2019) and van Staveren (2001, 2007). It is a perspective that takes up the distinction between the economic (*oikonomikê*) and chrematistics (*chrematistikê*) proposed by Aristotle.

The economic is thought by Aristotle "in opposition and in connection" with chrematistics (Crespo, 2017b, p. 261). Both are conceptualised in terms of wealth, but while the first refers to its use with a view to the realisation of a good life, the second refers to its production or acquisition. Aristotle further distinguished two kinds of chrematistics: one subordinated to the economic, aimed at the provision of the goods required for the good life, which is natural and necessary; the other, unnatural and unnecessary, consisting of the accumulation of wealth for its own sake. The distinction between the two has to do with the purposes for which they are realised. Whilst the former has as its aim the provision of the wealth necessary for the good life, the latter aims at the accumulation of goods and property.

One of the main ideas underpinning this re-reading of Aristotle within economics is the underlying assumption of the ontological priority of the community regarding the individual, given that human beings cannot flourish alone and such flourishing only happens in community (Crespo, 2017a, pp. 122–123). According to Polanyi (1947, pp. 201–202):

> Aristotle was right: man is not an economic, but a social being. He does not aim at safeguarding his individual interest in the acquisition of material possession, but rather at ensuring social good-will, social status, social assets. He values possessions primarily as a means to that end. His incentives are of that "mixed" character which we associate with the endeavor to gain social approval—productive efforts are no more than incidental to this. *Man's economy is, as a rule, submerged in his social relations.* The change from this to a society which was, on the contrary, submerged in the economic system was an entirely novel development.

Referring to the distinction between the economic and chrematistics and to the great thinkers of the twentieth century, Gerber (2016) considers two of the most important and well-known European institutionalists of the twentieth century, Karl William Kapp and Karl Polanyi, as major names in the study of the economic and of economics. The statement made by Kapp in 1954, with reference to Polanyi, regarding the need for economics to take as a point of departure "man's actual needs and his dependence upon and interaction with his natural and social environment" if it is to be "relevant for the interpretation of actual relationships and sequences of events under concrete historical and institutional conditions" (Kapp, 1954, p. 4), has great adherence to the current reality. For Kapp, the minimisation of human suffering and the sustainability of human life on our planet were the moral imperative of economics and economic policy (Luzzati, 2009, p. 318). It is a view which, like that of Perroux, also places man at the epicentre of the economy.

One must stress that the actual needs of man to be considered are not limited to basic physical needs. The absences of hunger, cold, or illness are crucial for someone to flourish, and, in this perspective, the provision of such basic needs is required for anyone to be able to flourish (Pirgmaier, 2020). However, such a provision is not enough. In the wake of Amartya Sen and Martha Nussbaum, among others, Pirgmaier (2020, p. 279) argues that the essential needs "that unite us as human beings" are health, autonomy, and connection. This researcher emphasises that it is essential that we "feel free and connected" to ensure that we are able to be "ourselves-in-community" and to feel "free-in-connection" (ibid.).

2.2 Ethics

In the first instance, ethics can be broadly understood as being concerned with the role of human values, the forms of behaviour that human beings assume in relation to each other and how we should live and live together (Wilde, 1998). But this is a very broad view of ethics. Bearing in mind the theme of the book that is offered to a wider audience, it is appropriate to present a more specific definition of ethics.

The starting point for the discussion that follows is Paul Ricoeur's understanding of ethics, as condensed in his conception of what he calls "ethical intention". Such ethical intention is defined by this philosopher as "aiming at the 'good life' with and for others in just institutions" (Ricoeur, 1992, p. 172). Regarding just institutions, Ricoeur (1992, p. 194) considers that "living well is not limited to interpersonal relations but extends to the life of institutions" and defines institution as "the structure of living together as this belongs to a historical community—people, nation, region, and so forth—a structure irreducible to interpersonal relations and yet bound up with these".

Ricoeur's understanding of ethics is not, however, sufficiently explicit regarding a crucial aspect today, that of the ecological problem. As Vandenberghe (2018, p. 94) observes, the issue of the intention of a sustainable environment is not considered in Ricoeur's phrase. But it is currently recognised to an increasingly unanimous degree as an indispensable condition for the survival of humanity and, "therefore, also of the good life in and with nature in an ecologically sustainable form of life" (ibid.). Therefore, I will retain the definition proposed by Renouard (2015) as it adds this latter issue to that of Ricoeur while maintaining its spirit. This French economist and philosopher defines ethics as "the specific, personal and collective, pursuit of the good life, today and tomorrow, within just institutions, at the service of the social and ecological link" (p. 55).

In this vein, ethics is both an individual concern for each of us and a common concern for all of us, and its essential interest is to obtain the better life possible for each and everyone (Renouard, 2015). Ethical reflection should not be confused with a moralising and coercive discourse regarding individual behaviours. It is rather a reflection on the social and economic ills that afflict us, on their causes and, fundamentally, on ways to mitigate them and ways of obtaining personal lives and a common life as good as possible. But ethics also has to do with the action taken to pursue these goals. In this perspective, whether it is understood as a concept, a challenge to companies, a field of action or a field of academic study (Carroll et al., 2012, p. 6), CSR is a participant in the pursuit for the good life.

2.3 Development

Taking up François Perroux's view of development presented above and relating it to the notions of sustainable development and human development that are so widespread today, CSR can be seen as corresponding to the contribution of corporations to sustainable human development.

I subscribe to the perspective that what one seeks to sustain when one has sustainable development as an objective is not so much the natural world as humanity itself (Sen, 2013). It is relatively obvious that a crucial aspect of sustainable development is human development. In the wake of Anand and Sen (2000), I see no difficulty in defining human development in such a way as to accommodate the interests of future generations and the urgency of protecting the natural world. Human development is not and cannot be anything other than sustainable development. As Klugman states (2010, p. 19),

> Human development is about enabling people to lead long, healthy, educated and fulfilling lives. Sustainable human development is about making sure that future generations can do the same. Human development, if not sustainable, is not true human development.

The notion of sustainable human development is adopted here largely because it is the one that is compatible with having as a goal the development of each person and of all people. On the basis of the work of Anand and Sen mentioned above, "sustainable human development" is defined by Klugman (2011, p. 20) as "the expansion of the substantive freedoms of people today while making reasonable efforts to avoid seriously compromising those of future generations".

It is the concept of "development as freedom", developed by Amartya Sen, and the capabilities approach, whose main promoters are Sen and Martha Nussbaum, that are at the basis of this notion of sustainable human development. McDonald (2006), who considers the concept of sustainable human development as the most suitable conceptual framework to comprehend sustainable development, argues that when most environmentalists refer to sustainable development, what they have in mind is such a concept.

Important concepts in the capability approach are those of functionings and capability. From Sen's perspective, human well-being is defined in terms of human functionings, and the concept of capability is defined in terms of functionings. Functionings are "the various things a person may value doing or being", and range from "elementary ones", such as being healthy and adequately nourished, to "complex activities or personal states, such as being able to take part in the life of the community and having self-respect" (Sen, 1999, p. 75). Regarding capability, Sen refers to it as "the substantive freedom to achieve alternative functioning combinations" (ibid.). It is the "opportunity to achieve valuable combinations of human functionings—what a person is able to do or be" (Sen, 2005, p. 153).

Based on Aristotelic ideas and the capabilities approach, Crespo (2013a, p. 62) presents the following shortlist of capabilities that he considers could be accepted by Sen:

i. Having the basic means for sustaining life.
ii. Being able to sustain oneself not through 'over-assistance', but through one's own property and work.
iii. Access to education.
iv. Access to law and justice.
v. Being able to participate in the political system.
vi. Being able to undertake initiatives concerning personal aims such as family, education, friendship, arts, religion, charity and, especially, virtues of all kinds.

In one of Sen's most recent works, on "the idea of justice", in which the capabilities approach plays a central role when referring to the relationship between such an approach and the concept of sustainable development, Sen (2009, pp. 251–252) states that

> If the importance of human lives lies not merely in our living standard and need-fulfilment, but also in the freedom that we enjoy, then the idea of sustainable development has to be correspondingly reformulated. There is cogency in thinking not just about sustaining the fulfilment of our needs, but more broadly about sustaining—or extending—our freedom (including the freedom to meet our needs). Thus recharacterised, sustainable freedom can be broadened from the formulations proposed by Brundtland and Solow to encompass the preservation, and when possible expansion, of the substantive freedoms and capabilities of people today 'without compromising the capability of future generations' to have similar— or more—freedom.

In this passage, Sen is referring to the definitions offered in the so-called Bruntlandt Report and by Robert Solow, recipient of the 1987 *Sveriges Riksbank* Prize in Economic Sciences in Memory of Alfred Nobel. The former has become the most widely used definition of sustainable development and offers a depiction of it as development that makes it possible to meet "the needs of the present without compromising the ability of future generations to meet their own needs" (Sen, 2009, pp. 249–250). Regarding Solow, Sen (2009, p. 250) considers that he has refined and extended the Brundtland Report's definition by considering as a fundamental requirement that the future generation is left with enough to "achieve a standard of living at least as good as our own and to look after their next generation similarly".

Regarding the understanding of sustainable development offered in the Brundtland Report, Sen (2009, p. 250) questions whether "the conception of human beings implicit" in it is based on a sufficiently "capacious view of humanity". As Sen states, "certainly people do have needs, but they also have values and, in particular, cherish their ability to reason, appraise, choose, participate and act" (ibid.). From this perspective, "seeing people only in terms of their needs may give us a rather meagre view of humanity" (ibid.).

Concerning Solow's proposal, when compared to that of the Brundtland Report, Sen acknowledges the merits of (1) going beyond the mere satisfaction of needs by emphasising the sustainability of living standards; (2) taking into consideration the interests of all future generations, by proposing a recursive formulation that attributes to each generation responsibilities towards the next. Notwithstanding, Sen questions whether "the coverage of standards of living is sufficiently inclusive", given that the reasons for valuing "particular opportunities" do not always lie in "their contribution to our living standards, or more generally to our own interests" (Sen, 2009, p. 250).

From Sen's perspective (2009, p. 250), on the contrary, "we are not only 'patients' whose needs deserve consideration, but also 'agents' whose freedom to decide what to value and how to pursue what we value can extend far beyond our own interests and needs". This is a perspective based on improving the ability to achieve what people have reason to value. Human beings are not mere consumers, who have only needs to be satisfied, but rather agents who value certain freedoms (concerning nutrition, health, literacy, security, political participation, etc.) and seek to achieve them. Sustainable human development is then the development that promotes the freedoms and capabilities of current generations without compromising the freedoms and capabilities of future generations (Sen, 2013).

References

Anand, S., & Sen, A. (2000). Human development and economic sustainability. *World Development, 28*(12), 2029–2049.

Carroll, A. B., Lipartito, K. J., Post, J. E., & Werhane, P. H. (2012). *Corporate responsibility: The American experience*. Cambridge University Press.

Crespo, R. F. (2013a). *Theoretical and practical reason in economics: Capacities and capabilities*. Springer.

Crespo, R. F. (2013b). *Philosophy of the economy: An Aristotelian approach*. Dordrecht: Springer.

Crespo, R. F. (2017a). *Economics and other disciplines: Assessing new economic currents*. London: Routledge.

Crespo, R. (2017b). L'ontologie de l'économie selon Aristote et la théorie économique actuelle. In G. Campagnolo & J. S. Gharbi (Eds.), *Philosophie Économique, un État des Lieux* (pp. 259–281). Paris: Éditions Matériologiques.

Crespo, R. F. (2019). Aristotle's principles for modern economic science. *Studia Gilsoniana, 8*(4), 819–837.

Gerber, J. F. (2016). The legacy of K. William Kapp. *Development and Change, 47*(4), 902–917.

Kapp, K. W. (1954). Economics and the behavioral sciences. In J. E. Ullmann & R. Preiswerk (Eds.), *The humanization of the social sciences* (pp. 1–20). University Press of America.

Klugman, J. (2010). *Human development report 2010 – 20th Anniversary Edition. The real wealth of nations: Pathways to human development.* United Nations Development Programme.

Klugman, J. (2011). *Human development report 2011. Sustainability and equity: A better future for all.* United Nations Development Programme.

Luzzati, T. (2009). Human needs, sustainable development, and public policy: Learning from K.W. Kapp (1910–1976). In N. Salvadori & A. Opocher (Eds.), *Long-run growth, Social institutions and living standards* (pp. 306–322). Edward Elgar.

Maréchal, J. P. (2003). L'héritage négligé de François Perroux. *L'Économie Politique, 4*, 47–63.

McDonald, R. (2006). Sustainable development as freedom. *International Journal of Sustainable Development & World Ecology, 13*(6), 445–447.

Perroux, F. (2010). *A new concept of development: Basic tenets.* Routledge.

Pirgmaier, E. (2020). Consumption corridors, capitalism and social change. *Sustainability: Science, Practice and Policy, 16*(1), 274–285.

Polanyi, K. (1947). Our obsolete market mentality. Civilisation must find a new thought pattern. In K. Polanyi (Ed.), *Economy and society: Selected writings* (pp. 197–2011). Wiley.

Renouard, C. (2015). *Éthique et Entreprise.* Éditions de l'Atelier.

Ricoeur, P. (1992). *Oneself as another.* University of Chicago Press.

Sen, A. (1999). *Development as freedom.* Alfred A. Knopf.

Sen, A. (2005). Human rights and capabilities. *Journal of Human Development, 6*(2), 151–166.

Sen, A. (2009). *The idea of justice.* Harvard University Press.

Sen, A. (2013). The ends and means of sustainability. *Journal of Human Development and Capabilities, 14*(1), 6–20.

Vandenberghe, F. (2018). Sociology as practical philosophy and moral science. *Theory, Culture & Society, 35*(3), 77–97.

Van Staveren, I. (2001). *The values of economics: An Aristotelian perspective.* Routledge.

Van Staveren, I. (2007). Beyond utilitarianism and deontology: Ethics in economics. *Review of Political Economy, 19*(1), 21–35.

Wilde, L. (1998). *Ethical Marxism and its radical critics.* London: Springer.

Chapter 3
The Corporation

Abstract In this chapter the view of the corporation that underpins the perspective on CSR upon which this book rests is presented. Similar to the previous one, this chapter helps setting the stage for the subsequent discussion of the issues on which this book focuses. The dominant theories of the corporation (the artificial entity, real entity, and aggregate theories) are presented, and a more recent theory—the collaboration theory of the corporation—is introduced as an attempt to address the shortcomings of the former theories. This latter theory, proposed by Eric Chaffee, is presented as especially interesting for the purpose of analysing the fight against corruption and responsible tax behaviour as CSR issues.

Keywords Corporation · Artificial entity theory · Aggregate theory · Real entity theory · Collaboration theory

Any meaningful discussion of CSR requires addressing the issue of what a corporation is, as the view of CSR one has depends on the view of the corporation one upholds (Avi-Yonah, 2008). Different views have different implications for the legitimacy of CSR (Avi-Yonah, 2014; McCredie & Sadiq, 2019).

First, I should note that what I have in mind when I refer to the corporation is an organisation formally recognised by law (a legal entity, therefore) established to produce and market goods and/or services. Although often used interchangeably, the terms "firm" and "corporation" do not refer to the same reality (Deakin, 2012; Robé, 2020). Whereas the firm is an organisation "engaged in the production of goods or services, to which end it combines physical, human and virtual assets", the corporation is "a legal mechanism, and the principal legal-institutional device through which business firms operate in contemporary market economies" (Deakin, 2012, p. 350). Notwithstanding, in what follows, I will use interchangeably the terms "company", "firm", "enterprise", and "corporation" to refer to the corporation as defined by Deakin. It is also important to note that calling shareholders owners of the corporation is something that economists usually do, but this results from a loose use of language, given that what they own are shares issued by corporations (Robé,

M. Castelo Branco, *Corporate Social Responsibility, the Fight Against Corruption and Tax Behaviour*, CSR, Sustainability, Ethics & Governance,
https://doi.org/10.1007/978-3-662-63735-7_3

2020). For ease of writing and because it is usual to do so, I will refer to the owners of corporations below, albeit the reader has to recall this caveat when I do so.

Perhaps the most interesting debate on the different views of the corporation is the one that legal scholars have been carrying out in recent decades regarding the legal personality of companies, namely because it has been carried out with reference to CSR and the relationship between CSR and tax behaviour (Avi-Yonah, 2004, 2005, 2008, 2014; Avi-Yonah & Sivan, 2007; Chaffee, 2019; Lan & Heracleous, 2010; Mann et al., 2019; McCredie & Sadiq, 2019; Munisami, 2018; Petrin, 2013; Padfield, 2015, 2017; Phillips, 1994a, 1994b, 1995). Padfield (2015, p. 19) goes so far as to state that these theories "seek to define the nature of corporations so as to provide a framework within which to determine the rights and responsibilities of corporations vis-à-vis the rest of society". It is because of their use in the analysis of CSR in general and its relationship with taxation and corporate tax behaviour that this book includes a brief discussion of some corporate personality theories.

3.1 The Dominant Theories of the Corporation

Within the debate on the legal personality of the corporation, three dominant views are usually identified (Avi-Yonah, 2004, 2005, 2008, 2014; Avi-Yonah & Sivan, 2007; Lan & Heracleous, 2010; McCredie & Sadiq, 2019; Panayi, 2015; Petrin, 2013; Padfield, 2015, 2017; Phillips, 1994a, 1994b, 1995): the artificial entity theory; the real entity theory; and the aggregate theory. The first of these views sees the type of organisation under consideration as an artificial entity, as a creature of the state. The second view conceives it as a real entity, an entity that is simultaneously separate from the state and from its owners. The third approach apprehends the corporation as the aggregate of its individual members or owners. As will be seen below, these different perspectives give rise to different approaches to CSR. In what follows, I refer to the business reality characteristic of modern capitalism. In addition to these three theories, also because of the relevance of its implications for the discussion of the topics addressed in this book, in particular, that of tax behaviour (Chaffee, 2019), a fourth theory recently developed by Chaffee (2016, 2017, 2019, 2020) will be introduced here.

Looking at the corporation as an artificial entity implies recognising that it owes its existence to the state, which not only grants it certain privileges (such as legal personality and limited liability) but also creates the conditions for its operations, through, for example, national defence and a regime of property rights, or even through the construction of infrastructure and the provision of health and education services to workers. And this is so because the corporation is created to perform a number of functions that are considered desirable. The corporation is seen as "a state creation intended to serve society at large under the umbrella of an active and engaged regulatory scheme" (Padfield, 2015, p. 20). From this perspective, involvement in some forms of CSR is part of the corporation's function. For example, to the extent that a corporation's activities result in damage to society, such as pollution, it has an obligation to remedy them.

The aggregate theory of the corporation is often associated with the modern view of the corporation as a nexus-of-contracts (or contractarian) view of the corporation (Padfield, 2017). For Watson (2019, p. 159), the aggregate theory is at the basis of current "law-and-economics" theories that conceive of the corporation as a nexus-of-contracts. Gindis (2009) refers to Jensen and Meckling's theory of the firm as a nexus-of-contracts and Grossman and Hart's theory of the firm as a collection of assets as modern recoveries of the aggregate theory. If we think of the corporation as an aggregate of its members, as a nexus-of-contracts, the only legitimate function of a firm is the maximisation of profits for the owners. From this perspective, engagement with CSR-related activities that are not related to profit maximisation is seen as a tax imposed by managers on the owners of the corporation.

If, on the contrary, we see the corporation as a real entity, it is considered as similar to an individual citizen in terms of rights and obligations. From this perspective, the corporation is seen neither as an aggregate of its owners nor as an extension of the state but rather as a separate entity controlled by its managers. As with any individual citizen, the corporation is not required to engage in activities beneficial to society other than those concerning its business, although such involvement is commendable and should be encouraged.

The aggregate and real entity theories of the corporation are undoubtedly the most popular ones nowadays. Nevertheless, the artificial entity theory has its contemporary defenders (Dibadj, 2012; Padfield, 2014, 2015). Referring to the decline of the artificial entity theory, Dibadj (2012) argues that it is related to an anti-regulatory fervour, coupled with the desire to elevate the managerial class in society that goes with it. According to this author, more than logical reasons, the reasons explaining the rise of the aggregate and the real entity theories of the corporation are instrumental reasons.

Although recognising some validity to each of those three theories, Chaffee (2016, 2017, 2019, 2020) considers that none of them offers a complete description or definition of what a corporation is. While the artificial entity theory ultimately underestimates the role of individuals in the organisation, operation, and ownership of the corporation and minimises the identity of the corporation as a collective of individuals and the state acting together, the aggregate theory minimises the role of the state in creating the corporation by focusing on the individuals who organise, operate, and own it and the relationships between them. The real entity theory, on the other hand, by focusing on the company as a distinct entity, underestimates the role of the state in the creation of the company and that of individuals in its organisation, operation, and ownership. Moreover, all these approaches focus on the question "*how* corporations exist", without offering any answer to another fundamental question, that of "*why* corporations exist". Although they are all convincing in that they "describe some aspect of the corporate form", none of them can provide "a robust definition of what is a corporation" (Chaffee, 2019, p. 101).

3.2 The Collaboration Theory of the Corporation

Attempting to address the shortcomings of the dominant theories of the corporation presented above, Chaffee (2016, 2017, 2019, 2020) proposes what he calls "collaboration theory", presenting the corporation as a collaboration between the government and the individuals who organise, operate, and own it (the "how corporations exist" aspect), to pursue the development of a common project, namely economic development and economic gain (the "why corporations exist" aspect). The objectives of the government and those of the individuals involved in such collaboration are not necessarily aligned. While the government seeks social-economic development and gain, individuals seek their own economic development and gain. However, because "in a representative democracy, the government represents the interests of the members of that society," when in such a society the government collaborates with the individuals who organise, operate, and own a corporation, this latter organisation has an obligation to become involved in a socially responsible manner because it is indebted to the government of that society for its existence (Chaffee, 2017, p. 350). Moreover, these individuals have "the obligation to pursue socially responsible behavior because the contractual nature of a corporation creates a fiduciary duty of good faith among the collaborating parties to treat each other well within the terms of the deal that they have struck in regard to creation and operation" of the entity concerned (ibid.). For Chaffee (2017, p. 369), a corporation treating the state government well is tantamount to behaving in a way that supports the well-being of society, i.e. "in a way that is socially responsible", since in a representative democracy the government is supposed to "represent the will of the people, which can be interpreted as the will of society".

Two important features of collaboration theory must be emphasised (Chaffee, 2016, 2017, 2019, 2020). First, going one step further than the real entity theory, collaboration theory argues that, because the corporation allows the individuals and entities that compose it to achieve more than they could by working separately, the corporation should be viewed as having a separate entity status from the entities and the individuals who facilitate its existence. Second, collaboration theory also explains why governments possess the ability to regulate corporations' rights. The individuals and entities that compose the collaboration that is the corporation have the ability to determine its existence. In the case of the government, this is done by way of law and regulation. Under such a conception of the corporation, "individuals retain their rights to fully and freely associate, but the state and federal governments retain the ability to determine with whom they want to collaborate" (Chaffee, 2016, p. 1761).

Collaboration theory "may offer the best hope when it comes to theories of corporate personhood" for those who want to further the cause of CSR (Padfield, 2017, pp. 448–449). For Padfield, with respect to the other three theories addressed, the characterisation proposed by Chaffee differentiates the collaboration theory by imposing the requirement for corporations to pursue pro-social objectives "whenever the expected value of a transaction is unknowable" or the pro-social action at

Table 3.1 Models of corporate governance

Models	Outline of the model	Supporting theories
Managerial model	Management is the corporate strategic Centre in a bureaucratic hierarchy, acting as a rational, self-disciplined mechanism. It is composed of expert professionals carrying out the objective implementation of shareholders' wishes.	Real entity theory
Director primacy model	The board of directors is a central, independent decision-maker for the firm. It mediates competing interests among the various groups that bear residual risk and have residual claims over the firm, and it allocates team surpluses.	Aggregate theory
Shareholder primacy model	Shareholders are the main residual claimants of the firm's income stream and have ultimate control over the corporation. The sole purpose of management is to maximise shareholders' wealth, and it should only engage in activities that are financially beneficial to shareholders.	Aggregate theory
Stakeholder/communitarian model	Nonshareholder constituencies have stakes in the corporation that are as equally important as those of shareholders. Managers and directors should be sensitive to stakeholders' interests when making decisions.	Artificial theory/ collaboration theory

Source: Adapted from Lan and Heracleous (2010, p. 299)

hand is neutral in terms of its impact on shareholder wealth (ibid.). I would add, even in some cases in which it is detrimental to shareholders, but this will be discussed in the next chapter.

Lan and Heracleous (2010) suggest that the three dominant theories presented above support different models of corporate governance: the aggregate theory supports shareholder primacy and director primacy models; the real entity theory supports a managerial model; the artificial theory supports a stakeholder/communitarian model. I put forward that collaboration theory also supports a stakeholder/ communitarian model, albeit with a lower emphasis on the role of the government. In Table 3.1, an outline of each of these models is offered.

The theory of collaboration also meets Petrin's (2013) criticisms of the three traditional theories discussed above and his proposal to define the corporation by its function rather than by its nature. For this researcher, the question should not be "what are firms?" but rather "why do we have firms?" and "how do they affect us?" (p. 32). In this regard, Petrin clearly states that "economic considerations are only one, albeit important, aspect of the firm" (p. 46). The impacts of business on society are considerable, and they can be positive or negative, and some of them are "intertwined with economic consequences" (ibid.). They range from "the creation and destruction of jobs and wealth" to "changes in everyday behavior or even broader cultural shifts" and include "impacts on health, safety, and the environment" and technological progress (ibid.). From Petrin's (2013) perspective, the increasingly important social impacts of business should be taken into account in developing a contemporary understanding of the corporation and should, in combination with economic considerations, contribute to the way in which the rights and duties of such entities are thought of.

Collaboration theory is especially interesting for our purpose of analysing two topics that are related to the economic dimension of CSR, which we can call economic responsibility. Such responsibility is understood in this book as referring to "a productive project that determines the allocation of resources and generates spill-over effects, the constitution of growth poles, the development of investments, job creation, innovation and the development of new skills" (Capron & Quairel-Lanoizelée, 2015, p. 81). This is a perspective according to which the company is accountable to society and its responsibility involves contributing to "the expenses and infrastructures of the states from which it benefits" (p. 84). According to the collaboration theory, this is a common project towards the pursuance of which the government and the individuals who organise, operate, and own the corporation collaborate. This entails also considering the corporation as a political actor.

3.3 The Corporation as a Political Actor

As Bommier and Renouard (2018, p. 34) state, to identify "the freedoms—and responsibilities—that the state grants to corporations in the process of creating value", it is necessary "to study how the corporation is defined and what its purpose is". These authors put forward that there are two major opposing views confronting each other on the relationship of the corporation to the law. The first, which has been the prevailing one for a long period, apprehends the company "as a *private* actor, that submits itself to state laws" and evolves according to its own ethical criteria and economic interests. The second view "apprehends the corporation as a political actor, with direct responsibility for the preservation (the 'impact' perspective) and the construction (the 'citizen' perspective) of a common good that supplants its financial interest" (ibid.).

This second conception of the corporation encompasses approaches that perceive the enterprise as a community, such as Solomon's (2004) Aristotelian view of the corporation, as well as Deakin's (2012) and Bommier and Renouard's (2018, 2019) views of the corporation as "commons". I view the collaboration theory as also encompassed within this view of the corporation as a political actor, which, at the same time, is a community and belongs to a community, and has direct responsibility for the preservation and the construction of the common good. All these approaches are, in my view, consistent with each other and, combined, offer an adequate view of the corporation.

For Solomon (2004), the fundamental principle of the Aristotelian approach to ethics in business is the recognition that corporations are fundamentally communities, people working together in the pursuance of common goals. An important implication of viewing the corporation as a community is the impossibility of conceiving it as a mere set of individuals focused only on their own interests.

From this perspective, the corporation "is itself a citizen, a member of a larger community and inconceivable without it" (p. 1028). Moreover, corporations "are part and parcel of the communities that created them, and the responsibilities that they bear are not the products of argument or implicit contracts but intrinsic to their very existence as social entities" (p. 1029).

The view of the corporation to which I adhere in this book is consistent with that proposed by Bommier and Renouard (2018, 2019), who conceive the corporation as a collective invested in a project at the service of the common good. In this perspective, the corporation can be characterised as follows:

- It is an "«external» political actor" in view of its power to intervene and shape issues pertaining to public service. This includes positive interventions, such as those pertaining to the training of its employees or their pensions, but also negative ones, such as the lobbying for regulations that are beneficial to business but harmful to society, mentioned in the introductory chapter.
- It is an "«internal» political actor". Being a community of individuals presenting diverse characteristics, including conflicting aspirations, concerns, and interests, the corporation is also "an arena of socialisation and experimentation of the collective" (Bommier & Renouard, 2018, p. 194). Independently of how vicious its internal politics is, the corporation is still a community, rather than a "mere collection of self-interested individuals" (Solomon, 2004, p. 1027). Here, one must refer to the classic confrontation between the workforce and the managers, with the latter trying to extract as much labour as possible from the former while paying them as little as possible. It is also regarding conflicts such as this that the state, as a full-fledged member of the collective, intervenes. Sometimes, often for long periods of time, the state acts in favour (or even at the service) of one of the parties, rather than having as a goal the common good.
- It is also a "common-pool resource". Given that the corporation itself has no owners (remember that what shareholders own are the shares) and considering the two former characteristics, it can be conceived as a collective entity regarding which there are a plethora of claims to property that are often in tension. The corporation is "a collective entity recognised by a body of rights, customs, and official and nonofficial rules" (Bommier & Renouard, 2019). Here, Bommier and Renouard (2018, 2019) borrow a term coined by Elinor Ostrom, recipient of the 2009 *Sveriges Riksbank* Prize in Economic Sciences in Memory of Alfred Nobel.

It is important to note that the roles as an internal and external political actor are not unconnected. If one thinks of such important aspects as the length of the working day and the intensity of labour, one has to consider those two aspects. Albeit the negotiation between employer and employee plays a role, it is well known that struggles about the length of the working day have not been resolved throughout history without public policies, and these were the object of lobby pressures both from corporations and unions (Moos, 2021). This is also an example of the government as a full-fledged member of the collective or community that makes up the corporation.

References

Avi-Yonah, R. S. (2004). Corporations, society, and the state: A defense of the corporate tax. *Virginia Law Review, 90*(5), 1193–1255.

Avi-Yonah, R. S. (2005). The cyclical transformations of the corporate form: A historical perspective on corporate social responsibility. *Delaware Journal of Corporate Law, 30*(3), 767–818.

Avi-Yonah, R. S. (2008). Corporate social responsibility and strategic tax behavior. In W. Schön (Ed.), *Tax and corporate governance* (pp. 183–198). Springer-Verlag.

Avi-Yonah, R. S. (2014). Corporate taxation and corporate social responsibility. *New York University Journal of Law & Business, 11*(1), 1–29.

Avi-Yonah, R. S., & Sivan, D. (2007). A historical perspective on corporate form and real entity. In Y. Biondi, A. Canziani, & T. Kirat (Eds.), *The firm as an entity: Implications for economics, accounting and the law* (pp. 153–185). Routledge.

Bommier, S., & Renouard, C. (2018). *L'Entreprise Comme Commun: Au-Delà de la RSE*. Éditions Charles Léopold Mayer.

Bommier, S., & Renouard, C. (2019). Corporate responsibility in the climate crisis. Books and Ideas. Accessed Jan 27, 2020, from https://booksandideas.net/Corporate-Responsibility-in-the-Climate-Crisis.html

Capron, M., & Quairel-Lanoizelée, F. (2015). *L'entreprise dans la société, une question politique*. La Découverte.

Chaffee, E. C. (2016). Collaboration theory: A theory of the charitable tax-exempt nonprofit corporation. *UC Davis Law Review, 49*(5), 1719–1781.

Chaffee, E. C. (2017). The origins of corporate social responsibility. *University of Cincinnati Law Review, 85*, 353–373.

Chaffee, E. C. (2019). Collaboration theory and corporate tax avoidance. *Washington & Lee Law Review, 76*, 93–162.

Chaffee, E. C. (2020). A theory of the business trust. *University of Cincinnati Law Review, 88*(3), 797–842.

Deakin, S. (2012). The corporation as commons: Rethinking property rights, governance and sustainability in the business enterprise. *Queen's Law Journal, 37*, 339–381.

Dibadj, R. (2012). (Mis) conceptions of the corporation. *Georgia State University Law Review, 29*, 731–782.

Gindis, D. (2009). From fictions and aggregates to real entities in the theory of the firm. *Journal of Institutional Economics, 5*(1), 25–46.

Lan, L. L., & Heracleous, L. (2010). Rethinking agency theory: The view from law. *Academy of Management Review, 35*(2), 294–314.

Mann, R., Martin, F., & Butcher, B. (2019). Saving the planet by cutting corporate taxes: A comparative case study analysis. *Florida Tax Review, 23*, 238.

McCredie, B., & Sadiq, K. (2019). CSR and tax: A study in the transition from an 'aggregate' to 'real entity' view of corporations. *Pacific Accounting Review, 31*(4), 553–573.

Moos, K. A. (2021). The political economy of state regulation: The case of the British factory acts. *Cambridge Journal of Economics, 45*(1), 61–84.

Munisami, K. (2018). The role of corporate social responsibility in solving the great corporate tax dodge. *Florida State University Business Review, 17*, 55–86.

Padfield, S. J. (2014). Rehabilitating concession theory. *Oklahoma Law Review, 66*, 327–361.

Padfield, S. J. (2015). Corporate social responsibility & concession theory. *William & Mary Business Law Review, 6*, 1–34.

Padfield, S. J. (2017). The role of corporate personality theory in opting out of shareholder wealth maximization. *Transactions: The Tennessee Journal of Business Law, 19*, 415–453.

Panayi, C. H. (2015). Is aggressive tax planning socially irresponsible? *Intertax, 43*(10).

Petrin, M. (2013). Reconceptualising the theory of the firm-from nature to function. *Penn State Law Review, 118*, 1–53.

Phillips, M. J. (1994a). Corporate moral personhood and three conceptions of the corporation. *Business Ethics Quarterly, 2*(4), 435–459.

Phillips, M. J. (1994b). Reappraising the real entity theory of the corporation. *Florida State University Law Review, 21*(4), 1061–1123.

Phillips, M. J. (1995). Corporate moral responsibility: When it might matter. *Business Ethics Quarterly, 5*(3), 555–576.

Robé, J. P. (2020). The shareholder value mess (and how to clean it up). *Accounting, Economics, and Law: A Convivium, 10*(3), 20190039.

Solomon, R. C. (2004). Aristotle, ethics and business organisations. *Organisation Studies, 25*(6), 1021–1043.

Watson, S. M. (2019). The corporate legal person. *Journal of Corporate Law Studies, 19*(1), 137–166.

Chapter 4
Corporate Social Responsibility

Abstract In this chapter the perspective on CSR upon which this book rests is presented. Similar to the previous two chapters, this one helps setting the stage for the subsequent discussion of the issues on which this book focuses. The concept of CSR is linked to sustainable human development. The typology of corporate responsibilities developed by Cécile Renouard (and colleagues) is presented. The implications of the theories of the corporation presented in the previous chapter to the analysis of the legitimacy of CSR are discussed. The main CSR-related instruments are presented, and the importance of non-financial reporting is discussed.

Keywords Corporate social responsibility · Corporate transparency · CSR-related instruments · Non-financial reporting · Theories of the corporation · Typologies of corporate responsibilities

4.1 Defining CSR

A definition of CSR according to which it is seen as "the responsibility of enterprises for their impact on society" (European Commission, 2011, p. 7) has been presented above. This definition corresponds to an update of the definition offered by the European Commission in the so-called Green Paper on CSR (European Commission, 2001), in which CSR is defined as a concept whereby corporations "decide voluntarily to contribute to a better society and a cleaner environment" (par. 8) or "integrate social and environmental concerns in their business operations and in their interaction with their stakeholders on a voluntary basis" (par. 20).

Following a consultation process on the Green Paper, the Commission published a follow-up document to the Green Paper and presented an EU strategy to promote CSR (European Commission, 2002). This second document summarises the results of a consultation process on the Green Paper and states that the positions expressed where significantly different. One example of such differences pertains to the views of corporations, on the one hand, and those of trade unions and civil society organisations, on the other hand. Corporations, for their part, "stressed the voluntary

M. Castelo Branco, *Corporate Social Responsibility, the Fight Against Corruption and Tax Behaviour*, CSR, Sustainability, Ethics & Governance,
https://doi.org/10.1007/978-3-662-63735-7_4

nature of CSR" and expressed the view that "attempts to regulate CSR at EU level would be counterproductive because this would stifle creativity and innovation among enterprises which drive the successful development of CSR" (p. 4). As for trade unions and civil society organisations, they stressed the inadequacy of voluntary initiatives to safeguard the rights of workers and citizens, advocating for the necessary regulatory framework to "establish minimum standards" and ensure a "level playing field" (ibid.). However, the definition originally proposed in the Green Paper was retained in this second document.

In the 2011 document in which the European Commission presented the definition of CSR adopted in this book as a starting point for discussion on this topic, CSR is defined without making direct and explicit reference to any voluntary character. Moreover, it is now considered that, in order to discharge such responsibility, respect for the applicable legislation and for collective agreements between parties is a matter of priority, i.e. such respect is "explicitly included in the definition" (Berger-Walliser & Scott, 2018, p. 188). This update of the definition has been related to the need felt by governments to move away from notions of CSR as being associated with voluntary activities beyond what is legally required at a time when CSR has become increasingly regulated (ibid.).

Although some authors consider the two concepts to be substantially different, albeit related (Meuer et al., 2020), the term CSR is used in this text as a synonym for corporate sustainability. Indeed, in the business sphere, the two terms are often used concurrently or as synonyms, both referring to the way companies integrate social, environmental, and governance considerations into their strategic and operational activities (Batruch, 2017, p. 445). Today, it is increasingly common to refer to environmental, social, and governance responsibilities and to use the acronym ESG (Environmental, Social, and Governance) to refer to the same realities that the two terms mentioned above also designate. In the wake of Matten and Moon (2004), the term CSR is used here as a kind of hat for this set of notions that seek to account for relations between business and society (such as, in addition to CSR, corporate citizenship or corporate sustainability) and business ethics. In this book, all these concepts are considered to refer to inextricable realities that concern the ethical role of corporations in society, which cannot but include their role in preserving resources for future generations.

Notwithstanding, in this regard, I find it important to note that, in the wake of Gray (2010, p. 57), I consider sustainability as both "an ecological and societal concept, which will only rarely, if at all, coincide with corporate or organisational boundaries". As put by Gray, it is a "systems-based concept" which, "environmentally at least, only begins to make any sense at the level of eco-systems and is probably difficult to really conceptualise at anything below planetary and species levels "(p. 48).

From this perspective, I advocate a reading of the relationship between the concepts of CSR and sustainable development similar to that presented by Rasche et al. (2017, p. 14), who mention that CSR has been seen by some as the contribution of business to sustainable development. The concept of sustainable development focuses on the development of society as a whole (or societies as a whole) rather than on the role of organisations (such as corporations) and adopts a macro-level perspective (ibid.). Moreover, such a perspective was the one adopted in the views of CSR proposed at the beginning of the twenty-first century by the European Commission and the World Business Council for Sustainable Development. The European Commission (2002) referred to CSR as the "contribution of business to sustainable development". In a pioneering and influential World Business Council for Sustainable Development paper on CSR, it was defined as "the commitment of business to contribute to sustainable economic development, working with employees, their families, the local community and society at large to improve their quality of life" (Holme & Watts, 2000, p. 10). Regarding this latter definition, two improvements I think one could introduce are: first, instead of referring to sustainable economic development, one should refer to sustainable human development; and, second, include the explicit reference to the government or the state as one of the entities with which corporations work with to ameliorate the quality of living. As mentioned in the previous chapter, I view the state as one of the manifold full-fledged members of the collective to which we call corporation.

CSR has to do with the responsibility corporations have for the economic, social, and environmental impacts of their activities. It concerns the consideration of ethical issues in corporate decision-making and behaviour, in particular with regard to the responsibility to perform certain actions and refrain from engaging in others. First, it concerns issues such as whether and how companies should act to prevent, mitigate, and remedy the negative effects of their activities (mitigating the environmental damage of their activities, combating corruption, etc.). Second, it is about whether and how they should act to ensure and enhance the positive effects associated with their business, for example, relative to paying their fair share of tax, contributing to local development, or even through the so-called base of the pyramid strategies.[1] Finally, it also has to do with whether and how they should act to enhance their positive impacts by engaging in activities not directly associated with their business, including promoting social well-being through their involvement in philanthropic activities.[2]

CSR concerns issues as diverse and complex as the environmental impacts of production processes and products, industrial relations, the relations with local communities, suppliers, and consumers, as well as with the society at large. These

---

[1] Base of the pyramid strategies are presented by Landrum (2014, p. 294) as those intending to target the poorest fringes of the population in developing countries and pursuing concomitantly the following three goals: produce and market environmentally, socially, and economically sustainable products using processes and models presenting this same characteristics; ameliorate the lives of such fringes of the population; and obtain benefits or profits for the corporation and other partners.

[2] In truth, CSR's most fundamental aspect today is how corporations make their profits. Some influential authors go as far as rejecting the inclusion of philanthropy in the concept of CSR (Hopkins, 2007; Heal, 2008). Lin-Hi (2010, p. 86) argues that "philanthropy is not a sensible focal point for CSR" and goes as far as claiming that "philanthropic activities, such as donations, sponsoring, etc., are economically useful and not entirely problematic, *as long as they are viewed as instruments of the classic marketing mix*" (p. 89).

issues encompass not only aspects pertaining to human rights, labour and employment practices, environmental impacts, corruption, and tax behaviour but also aspects concerning community involvement and consumer protection. What is more, the promotion of CSR through corporations' supply chain and the disclosure of information regarding how they engage with these issues are "important cross-cutting issues" (European Commission, 2011, p. 7).

Using loose language, one may say that CSR is about, on the one hand, how companies generate their profits (respecting their workers, respecting human rights, having concerns about the environmental impacts of processes and products, not getting involved in corruption practices, paying their fair share of taxes, etc.), and, on the other hand, how they use their resources beyond the core business (charitable contributions, etc.).

Renouard and Ezvan (2018) propose an interesting definition of CSR, which, according to these researchers, is consistent with the criteria set out by the European Commission in its 2011 document as well as with the capability perspective presented very briefly in Chap. 2. Above I depicted CSR as corporations' contribution to sustainable human development, stating that at the basis of this notion was the concept of "development as freedom" developed by Amartya Sen. CSR's definition proposed by Renouard and Ezvan (2018) is in line with this view of CSR. These researchers see CSR as "a responsibility towards human development in two complementary ways: (a) a holistic responsibility shared by companies together with other actors to safeguard humanity and (b) a direct liability of each company for its impact on stakeholders' capabilities" (p. 144).

These researchers also propose what I consider to be the most interesting typology of corporate social responsibilities, not least because tax behaviour is explicitly addressed and, although implicitly (as a political responsibility), the same is the case with the fight against corruption. As Renouard and Ezvan (2018, p. 147) point out, the definition of CSR (and the typology of responsibilities) they propose focuses "on the direct impacts of business on different kinds of stakeholders and integrates more explicitly issues related to the financial criteria of fair value sharing, taxation, and profit making in the realm of corporate responsibilities". The typology they propose is based on that proposed by Renouard (2015) and Bommier and Renouard (2018, 2019) and includes four main types or areas of responsibility, which are presented by Renouard and Ezvan (2018) as follows:

- "An economic and financial responsibility to consider profit as a means and humanity as an end.
- A social responsibility towards employees and subcontractors to enhance their central capabilities.
- A societal and environmental responsibility to fight against negative externalities that destroy human capabilities in the long term.
- A political responsibility to promote proactive voluntary cooperation towards structural and institutional changes, enabling people to get more control over their environment."

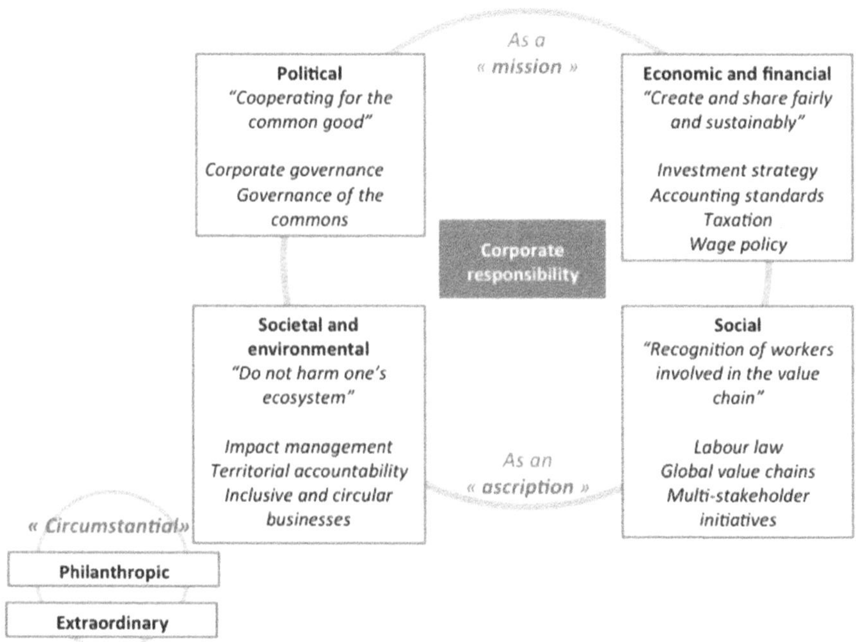

Fig. 4.1 The responsibilities of corporations. Source: Bommier and Renouard (2019)

Renouard (2012, 2015) and Bommier and Renouard (2018, 2019) consider, in addition, a philanthropic responsibility and an extraordinary responsibility (emergency assistance). These "circumstantial" or "subsidiary" responsibilities, in particular the extraordinary responsibility, have acquired a new relevance after the emergence of the Covid-19 pandemic. This latter responsibility has to do with the provision of assistance to people in danger and is relevant in situations of dire emergency. As an example of it, Renouard (2012, p. 65) refers to the mobilisation of corporations in the aftermath of the 2005 tsunami in Thailand and Indonesia to provide assistance to public authorities by supplying them with several types of resources. Bommier and Renouard (2019) offer a picture summarising this typology (Fig. 4.1).

This view of CSR is consistent with what Geva (2008) calls "concentric-circle model of CSR", which this researcher identifies as preferable to Archie Carroll's pyramid of CSR and the "intersecting circles model of CSR". Carroll (1991) presents a view of CSR according to which it encompasses four categories of responsibilities: economic, legal, ethical, and philanthropic. According to him, this set of CSR categories can be depicted as a pyramid, with the economic responsibility at the basis and the philanthropic responsibility at the apex. This model of CSR has been subsequently developed and transformed, namely by Schwartz and Carroll (2003), who proposed what Geva (2008) calls the "intersecting circles model of CSR".[3] It has also been applied to contexts such as the African (Visser, 2006, 2008, 2014).

Although acknowledging that Carroll's pyramid in some way negates the so-called separation thesis, according to which one can make a neat and sharp separation between the economy and ethics,[4] namely because it recognises that corporations can fulfil the four responsibilities simultaneously, Geva (2008) criticises it for not saying nothing about how the four responsibilities interwove. This researcher proposes a "concentric-circle model of CSR", which "outlines the non-economic social responsibilities as embracing and permeating the core economic responsibilities" (p. 22). According to such a view, rather than conceiving CSR as a mere aggregation of responsibilities, one should conceive it as "an entity or system made up of interrelated responsibilities, with mutual and reciprocal influence on each other", whose value as a whole is greater than that of the sum of its parts (p. 27).

By proposing the adoption of a concentric-circle model of CSR, Geva (2008, p. 27) is proposing us to view CSR "as a global concept whose parts are bound together by means of a shared intrinsic content, which can be defined as a commitment to operate in a way that promotes the good of society." According to this view of CSR, "all economic responsibilities also have legal and ethical aspects" (p. 23). Differently from the other two models identified by Geva, which adopt "a narrow definition of economic responsibility that focuses on the fundamental call on business to be a profit-making enterprise" (p. 24), the economic responsibility in the concentric-circle model of CSR:

> is not simply about wealth creation; it is about generating wealth that improves the nation's standard of living, supplying the needs and wants of people for goods and services, and selling them at fair prices, providing jobs and decent wages to the work force, expanding career opportunities in all parts of society, and eliminating poverty. Under this wide definition, profitability is not the critical test for economic responsibility. (ibid.)

It is interesting to note that Visser's (2006, 2008, 2014) use of Carroll's CSR pyramid in a developing country context led him to emphasise other aspects of the economic responsibility besides the profitability one. This researcher claims that in such a context, the focus of CSR tends to be on the so-called economic multipliers, which is a term that concerns aspects such as generating investment and income, producing safe products and services, creating jobs, investing in human capital, establishing local business linkages, spreading international business standards, supporting technology transfer, and building physical and institutional infrastructure. In the picture he offers as an adaptation of Carroll's CSR pyramid for developing countries, Visser mentions as economic responsibilities the provision of

---

[3]This model is not presented in detail here given that such presentation is not relevant for the argument I want to present.

[4]Freeman (1994, p. 412) refers to "a separation of the discourse of business from the discourse of ethics". I entirely agree with Harris and Freeman's (2008, p. 543) that "the problem with the separation thesis is not so much that it actually separates business and ethics—an impossible task—but that it purports moral neutrality while surreptitiously encapsulating certain ethical values and assertions."

investment, the creation of jobs, and the payment of taxes. In addition, instead of legal responsibilities, the second-highest priority is given to philanthropic responsibilities, followed by the legal and the ethical responsibilities. It is also worthy of note Crane et al.'s (2019, p. 53) call of attention to the fact that the focus on profit as an aspect of economic responsibility is a feature of the Anglo-American model and that this responsibility is defined rather more broadly in the European and Asian approaches, in which greater emphasis is placed on the economic responsibility towards employees and local communities.

4.2 Theories of the Corporation and CSR

Avi-Yonah (2005, 2008, 2014) develops an interesting approach to the implications of the three main theories of the corporation presented above for the legitimacy of CSR. For the purposes of the elaboration of Table 4.1, the collaboration theory developed by Chaffee (2016, 2017, 2019, 2020) has been added to the three main theories considered by Avi-Yonah.

Avi-Yonah (2014, p. 15) considers the first type of CSR as concerning activities that can "clearly and demonstrably benefit shareholders in the long run". He describes such activities as those which, although costly in the short term, can help prevent future events that may be disastrous for the company. Examples are activities designed to prevent environmental disasters or to respect legal and ethical rules. All theories consider these activities as legitimate.

The second type of CSR includes activities conceived to mitigate social damages regarding which the corporation bears responsibility for, "even when there is no direct legal liability and no demonstrable benefit to shareholders" (ibid.). This type of activity is not considered legitimate by the aggregate theory, as it does not benefit shareholders. For the artificial entity theory, however, because an implicit contract can be inferred according to which the corporation will help the state in the mitigation of the damage caused by it, even if there is no legal obligation to do so. The real entity theory also sees this type of activity as legitimate. Collaboration theory's response is not clear cut, as discussed below.

Table 4.1 Theories of the corporation and CSR

		Theory			
		Aggregate	Artificial	Real	Collaboration
Type of CSR	For long-run benefit of shareholders	Yes	Yes	Yes	Yes
	Not for shareholders	No	Yes	Yes	Yes[a]
	Not for shareholders, corporations not responsible	No	No	Yes	Yes[a]

[a]Considered as legitimate except when it is detrimental to profits
Source: Adapted from Avi-Yonah (2014, p. 15)

As for the third type of CSR, it concerns activities pertaining to issues for which no responsibility can be attributed to the corporation and, more often than not, does not directly benefit the shareholders. Avi-Yonah (2014, p. 15) gives as an example of the latter type of CSR the involvement in activities aimed at AIDS prevention. This type of CSR would not be considered legitimate according to the artificial entity theory and the aggregate theory. According to the real entity theory, since corporations are considered as persons, they would be allowed to engage in philanthropic activities as individuals would do. That is, according to the latter theory, even in the case of CSR activities not at all related to the obtention of benefits to shareholders or direct responsibility from the corporations are allowed. Again, collaboration theory's response is not clear cut, as discussed below.

Grounded on collaboration theory, Chaffee (2017, pp. 370–372) explores four scenarios to examine when a corporation has an obligation to engage in a socially responsible activity not legally mandatory. The first is that of such activity also being profitable to the corporation. The second pertains to a situation in which the socially responsible activity at hand is detrimental to profits. The third scenario concerns a setting in which the activity is financially neutral. In the fourth scenario, it is uncertain whether the activity under consideration is beneficial or deleterious to profits. According to Chaffee, only in the case of the second scenario should the corporation decline to engage in the activity at stake. Regarding scenarios three and four, the corporation has an obligation to engage in the socially responsible activity even in case it is not financially beneficial due to the duty it has of treating well the government and the society it represents in the collaboration. It is important to note, as Chaffee also does, that the third scenario "reflects the exceptional case in which the consequences" of corporations' behaviour are clear (2017, p. 372). I would add that most CSR activities, whose benefits are predominantly intangible and work via reputation, organisational commitment, and similar mechanisms, scenarios one to three are exceptional. In most cases, it is not possible to determine clearly the "cost-effective course of action" (ibid.).

Chaffee's account is different from that of Avi-Yonah. Whereas this latter author refers to whether the corporation is permitted to engage in certain socially responsible activities, Chaffe refers to whether the corporation is obliged to engage in certain socially responsible activities. However, Chaffe's account adds to that of Avi-Yonah the consideration of different scenarios in terms of impact on profits (the activity in consideration is beneficial, detrimental, neutral, or has an uncertain impact). Albeit it is not easy to combine the two approaches, and probably this should not be attempted, such an exercise will serve to enrich the discussion.

Avi-Yonah refers to not legally mandatory activities that are conceived to mitigate social damages for which the corporation bears responsibility and regarding which no demonstrable benefit accrues to shareholders. Considering Avi-Yonah's (2014, p. 15) explanation of activities that "demonstrably benefit shareholders in the long run", I am interpreting the situation described as one of the benefits of engaging in the activity not surpassing the associated costs. In terms of Chaffee's terminology, this would amount to a situation in which the activity is neutral, detrimental, or uncertain as to its impact on profits. Chaffe upholds that only when such impact is demonstrably deleterious can the corporation refrain from engaging in such an activity. In the other cases, it is obliged to do so. Avi-Yonah upholds that, in all three scenarios, only according to the aggregate theory the corporation is not permitted to engage in such activities.

Chaffee (2017, p. 371) puts forward the "disturbing" idea that "because of the collaboration forged with the government to promote economic growth, a for-profit corporation has an obligation to seek profit, even when it involves acting in a socially irresponsible manner". This idea allows Chaffe to emphasise "the importance of regulators in policing corporations" (ibid.). The state can impose costs to corporations related to their non-compliance with the law that would otherwise not exist and lead corporations to adopt responsible practices because not adopting them would be detrimental to profits (because of the costs of non-compliance with the law). I find this view of the state's role very important and put forward that in all situations regarding which the corporation bears responsibility for social harms, it should have legal responsibilities concerning its mitigation. This idea would, however, merit a more profound discussion that I will leave to future research in view of the introductory nature of this book.

Be that as it may, in the particular case of activities designed to mitigate social harms for which the corporation bears responsibility but regarding which it has no legal responsibility, because in most cases such social harms are detrimental to economic development and the state will have to bear the burden of mitigating them, I would argue that the corporation has an obligation to help the state and at least share such a burden. One would have to find a way to ascertain the point at which the costs of assisting the state in the mitigation of such harms would impair the contribution of the corporation for social-economic development and gain.

In effect, one of the aspects deserving further development is the idea that seeking profit is always tantamount to economic growth, to which Chaffee seems to adhere. Moreover, one has to discuss the possibility of seeking profit being detrimental to economic prosperity, even if it is beneficial to economic growth. This is an important discussion because one should not and cannot conflate the "economic development and economic gain" that Chaffee (2017, p. 365) claims to be the "common project" of the members of the corporation with economic growth. But I leave this discussion to another day.

Regarding the case of Avi-Yonah's third type of CSR, that of activities pertaining to issues for which no responsibility can be attributed to the corporation and, more often than not, do not directly benefit the shareholders, I submit that the corporation is never obliged to engage in such activities, although it can surely do so. This is because, at least in terms of an individual corporation's responsibility, I subscribe to a definition of CSR as responsibility for impacts on society, such as the ones proposed by the European Commission (2011) and Renouard and Ezvan (2018). Recalling Renouard and Ezvan's (2018, p. 144) definition of CSR, each corporation has a "direct liability" for the impacts it has on the capabilities of its stakeholders, and corporations as a whole have a "holistic responsibility", which they share "with other actors to safeguard humanity".

4.3 Main CSR Voluntary Instruments and Legislation

CSR voluntary instruments have multiplied in recent decades. They range from the instruments covering most of the aspects associated with CSR (such as the OECD Guidelines for MNEs, the UNGC, the GRI Standards, or the ISO 26000) to those focusing on specific aspects (such as the SA 8000, the ISO 14001, the Carbon Disclosure Project, or the United Nations Guiding Principles on Business and Human Rights). More recently, important pieces of CSR-related legislation have been passed, in particular, pertaining to CSR reporting, such as the so-called EU Non-Financial Reporting Directive (EU NFRD) and its subsequent transposition to national legislation. At this point, I will focus on CSR voluntary instruments and CSR legislation that cover most aspects of CSR. They will be presented only very briefly.

CSR voluntary instruments are often differentiated on the basis of:

(i) being based on shared principles and codes of practice (e.g., OECD Guidelines for Multinational Enterprises, UNGC);
(ii) corresponding to management systems and certification schemes (e.g., AA1000, SA8000, ISO 14001, ISO 26000)[5];
(iii) pertaining to CSR/sustainability reporting (e.g., the GRI Standards, the IIRC) (Arvidsson, 2019; Zinenko et al., 2015).

In presenting such instruments, one has to acknowledge that the "CSR movement" has benefited immensely from the efforts of some international organisations, which have launched important initiatives to promote CSR and its communication. Among them, the Organisation for Economic Cooperation and Development (OECD), the United Nations (UN), and the International Standardization Organization (ISO) stand out for their historical role.

According to Batruch (2017, p. 446), it was with the development of the OECD Guidelines for Multinational Enterprises in 1976 that CSR received its first mainstream validation. These guidelines were not intended to establish legal requirements, but rather "called upon companies to carry out their activities in an ethical way, with due regard to social and environmental issues" (ibid.). Although these guidelines have been revised several times, they remain an important benchmark for business conduct, not only for corporations but also for governments and investors (ibid.). Since their emergence in 1976, five revisions have been made to the OECD Guidelines, the last one dating from 2011. The OECD Guidelines for MNEs 2011 version addresses explicitly the following topics: Human Rights (chapter IV); Employment and Industrial Relations (chapter V); Environment (Chapter VI); Combating Bribery, Bribe Solicitation and Extortion (Chapter VII); Consumer Interests (chapter VIII); Science and Technology (chapter IX); Competition (chapter X), and Taxation (chapter XI). In addition to chapters on these topics, the OECD Guidelines

[5]Albeit ISO 26000 is not a management system standard and is not intended for certification purposes, I believe it can be included in this category.

for MNEs include chapters on Concepts and Principles (chapter I), General Policies (chapter II), and Disclosure (chapter III). Relative to the previous version, changes include the introduction of a human rights chapter and updates on topics such as employment and industrial relations, the environment, consumer interests, combating bribery, bribe solicitation and extortion, taxation, and disclosure.

At the level of the UN, two initiatives (which, in one way or another, it has promoted) stand out: the UNGC and the GRI. The UNGC (2008) was announced by former UN Secretary-General Kofi Annan at the World Economic Forum in Davos, Switzerland, in January 1999 and formally launched at UN headquarters in July 2000. It is a voluntary initiative that seeks to mobilise the business community around the concept of corporate citizenship by making it an active part of the solutions to change the process of globalisation. The UNGC corresponds to a network of diverse organisations created to promote certain values and objectives related to CSR. The signatories of the UNGC are committed to pursuing a set of 10 principles (pertaining to the issues of human rights, labour, environment, and corruption) conceived on the basis of international declarations and principles. In 2020, the Global Compact had more than 13,000 participants, 10,000 from business, and 3000 from civil society and non-business organisations, from more than 160 countries (DNV GL/UNGC, 2020).

The GRI is an initiative launched in 1997 by the United Nations Environment Programme (UNEP) in collaboration with the Coalition for Environmentally Responsible Economies (CERES) with the mission of developing and disseminating globally applicable guidelines/standards for organisations to use in sustainability reporting. The GRI guidelines propose namely a set of indicators that companies can use to provide information on economic, social, and environmental performance. The first draft of the guidelines was proposed in 1999, and a programme to test such guidelines was launched immediately. The first version of the guidelines was officially launched in 2000. The second version appeared in 2002 (G2), and the third was launched in 2006 (G3). In 2011 the G3.1 version was released, corresponding to an update of the G3 version. In 2013 the G4 version was published. In 2016 the GRI Standards were created (GRI, 2020). As of November 2020, these standards correspond to a set of 34 individual standards, each on a specific aspect. In addition to a set of universal standards that any organisation can use (on general disclosures and the management approach), it includes specific standards related to three aspects: the economic, the social, and the environmental. The standards on the economic aspect address topics such as economic performance (from a perspective of economic value generated and distributed), indirect economic impacts (e.g. infrastructure investments and impacts on local communities and economies), corruption, anti-competitive behaviour, tax, etc. The social standards are devoted to labour/management relations, diversity and equal opportunity, freedom of association and collective bargaining, rights of indigenous peoples, customer privacy, among many others. The environmental standards address issues such as materials, energy, and biodiversity. This is undoubtedly the best known and most widely used set of sustainability reporting guidelines worldwide.

Although it was formed in 1946, the ISO only began developing standards pertaining to management systems in the 1980s, with the ISO 9000 series (Sethi et al., 2017). ISO 26000 was established in 2010 with the purpose of providing guidance on managing CSR and explicitly considers the following core subjects: organisational governance, human rights, labour practices, environment, fair operating practices, community involvement and development, and consumer issues. Differently from the ISO 14000 and the ISO 9000, ISO 26000 is not certifiable.

Regarding CSR legislation, one cannot but emphasise the importance of the EU in its development. Although the issue of social responsibility had assumed some importance in the EU at least since the mid-1990s, when Jacques Delors (President of the European Commission at the time) called on European companies to help combat social exclusion, it has become a substantial issue mainly at the beginning of the twenty-first century (Orbie & Babarinde, 2008). Essential to its resurgence and definitive implementation were mainly the publications of the Green Paper "Promoting a European framework for Corporate Social Responsibility" in 2001 (European Commission, 2001) and the subsequent Communications of 2002 (European Commission, 2002) and 2006 (European Commission, 2006). Another milestone in the development of the EU's approach to CSR was the 2011 document "Corporate social responsibility: a new EU strategy for 2011-2014" (European Commission, 2011), which offers a new definition of CSR. In addition to these documents, one should mention the so-called Non-financial Reporting Directive (Directive 2014/95/EU of the European Parliament and of the Council) and, in the wake of this document, the communication of the Commission 2017/C 215/01 offering guidance on non-financial reporting (European Commission, 2017). Kinderman (2018, p. 109) considers the Directive 2014/95/EU as "the most important legacy of the EU's renewed strategy for CSR".

4.4 The Importance of Non-financial Reporting

NFR, the disclosure of non-financial information, which, as understood in this book, is nothing else but sustainability reporting (or CSR reporting) (possibly extended to include the so-called integrated reporting),[6] is perceived as an important

[6]A more comprehensive notion of what constitutes NFR would lead us to include in its scope other types of reporting besides sustainability reporting, such as, amidst others, intellectual capital reporting or risk reporting (Stolowy & Paugam, 2018; Tarquinio & Posadas, 2020). In this book I will take the most restrictive view of NFR, as it is the one that is used most often today. For example, Hess (2012) uses the term NFR as meaning the same as corporate social reporting or sustainability reporting, and Monciardini et al. (2020) use the term NFR as a synonym for social and environmental reporting, adding that such use is consistent with the European Commission's approach which focuses on information on environmental, social, and worker-related issues, human rights, and combating corruption and bribery. Notwithstanding, the best-known model of integrated reporting, the one proposed by the International Integrated Reporting Council (IIRC) (its initial version has been released in 2013 and its first revised version has been released in 2021)

cross-cutting issue of CSR. The disclosure of this type of information by corporations has become an increasingly important aspect of their CSR practices. Perhaps it is the surveys on this type of reporting carried out periodically by KPMG that offer the most relevant longitudinal depiction of the evolution of corporations' interest in CSR and its reporting. According to these surveys, CSR and its reporting have initially focused almost exclusively on one of its components, the environmental one. This had its reflections in terms of CSR reporting, which until about 1999 was almost exclusively environmental reporting and only since then has it truly become a more comprehensive (social, environmental, and economic) reporting (KPMG, 2005).

The most recent KPMG survey (KPMG, 2020) reports on the analysis of NFR by 5200 of the world's largest corporations, resulting from the selection of the top 100 corporations from 52 countries and jurisdictions (N100) and the top 250 Global Fortune 500 corporations (G250), with the G250 corporations largely corresponding to a subset of the N100 (only 23 of the G250 are not included in the N100, because they are not headquartered in the countries and jurisdictions reviewed). The data presented in this survey show a sustained increase in the disclosure of non-financial information (Fig. 4.2).

Concerning the G250 corporations, the reporting rate increased from 35% in 1999 to 96% in 2020, with the rate remaining more or less stable between 92% and 96% between 2011 and 2020. Regarding the N100 corporations, in the same period, the reporting rate increased from 24% to 80%. This type of development led KPMG (2017, p. 4) in its previous report to consider that this type of reporting had become "standard practice" worldwide for large and mid-cap corporations. In the 2020 report, KPMG refers to the "monumental changes" that have occurred since 1993 in the type of reporting in question and refers to its current state as one of almost universal adoption (p. 7). Another interesting development concerns the percentage of corporations that include sustainability information in their annual financial reports, which, after having increased between 2015 and 2017 from 56% to 60% in the case of N100, and from 65% to 78% in the case of G250 (KPMG, 2017), seems to have stabilised (in 2020, 61% in the case of N100, and 76% in the case of G250). The rates of independent verification of the type of information under analysis also showed sustained growth between 2005 and 2020: from 33% to 51% for N100 and from 30% to 71% for G250.

Despite the evidence provided by KPMG showing a favourable evolution of NFR from a quantitative point of view, other recent studies show a relative underdevelopment of such reporting from a qualitative point of view. For example, the results of the examination of the implementation of the EU Non-Financial Reporting Directive (Alliance for Corporate Transparency, 2020), which presents evidence regarding the

(IIRC, 2021), which proposes the integration of financial, sustainability, intellectual capital, risk and corporate governance information, will be treated as a sustainability reporting initiative, as Tsagas and Villiers (2020) do, although I have not considered it as one of the main instruments associated with CSR.

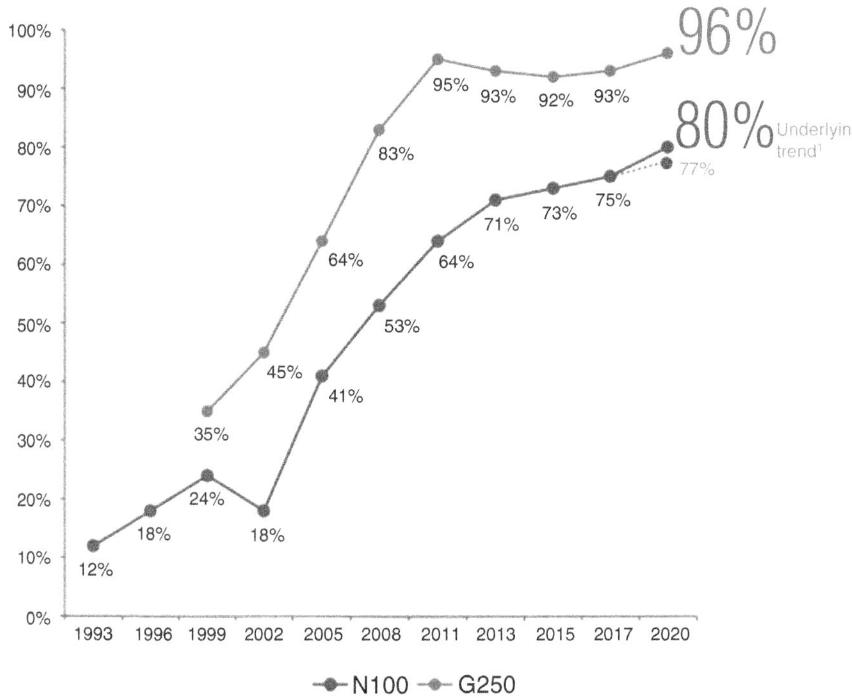

Fig. 4.2 Growth in the rates of NFR. Source: KPMG (2020, p. 10)

practices of this type of reporting of 1000 European companies, suggest that although such reporting is widespread (with 19 out of 20 companies reporting such information), there is a problem concerning companies reporting policies rather than results, which leads to the claim that there is a "failure to address concrete issues, targets and principal risks" (p. 4).

Today there are several organisations whose objective is the production of standards for NFR. GRI is the pioneer in this effort, and I have already referred to it. More recently, the Sustainability Accounting Standards Board (SASB) was established in the USA with a similar purpose (Busco et al., 2020). In 2011, the International Integrated Reporting Council (IIRC) was created, and the first version of its International Integrated Reporting Framework (IIRF) was published in 2013, being replaced by a revised version in 2021 (IIRC, 2021). There are also organisations not directly devoted to the task of proposing NFR standards that decided to intervene, such as the case of the World Economic Forum, which, in collaboration with the BIG 4 (Deloitte, EY, KPMG and PwC), has proposed a "core set of 'Stakeholder Capitalism Metrics' (SCM) and disclosures" (WEF, 2020, p. 3). Adams (2020, p. 194) refers to the report in which the WEF presented such a proposal as "providing little incentive for businesses to focus on adapting their strategy to make a positive contribution to sustainable development".

Monciardini et al. (2020) provide a historical perspective on NFR frameworks and standards, referring to three waves of such frameworks and standards. The first wave occurred essentially in the 1970s and was led by governments, resulting in the above-mentioned OECD Guidelines for MNEs. These researchers point out that in the early 1980s, the "international regulatory debate suddenly came to an end", with the result that "for over than two decades, non-financial disclosure was widely conceived as only a market-led practice, adopted by corporations on a purely voluntary and discretionary basis" (p. 13). In the late 1990s and early 2000s, the second wave of NFR frameworks and standards emerged. This second wave saw the emergence of the UNGC and the GRI, together with the Eco-Management and Audit Scheme (EMAS) (established in 1993) and the CDP (founded in 2000). As Monciardini et al. (2020, p. 13) point out, consistent with the prevailing spirit of the "retreat of the state" era, these frameworks and standards "are voluntary and often were filling the void due to the lack of legislative initiatives on" NFR. They also point out that underlying this second wave is the so-called business case for CSR and that, compared to the previous wave, there is "a stronger emphasis on climate and environmental issues" (of which EMAS and CDP are illustrations) (pp. 13–14). The third wave, the one we are in today, emerged after the 2008 crisis "in response to the legitimacy crisis of laissez-faire and voluntary approaches to business regulation that characterised the three decades between 1980 and 2010" (p. 14).

Regarding this third wave, in which new structures and standards have emerged, in particular the ISO 26000, the IIRF and the Sustainable Development Goals (SDGs) (2015), Monciardini et al. (2020) highlight three aspects. The first relates to the increased importance of public authorities in regulating NFR, as evidenced by the enactment of the NFR Directive and subsequent transposition into the national laws of its several member states at the EU level or, at the national level, the Dodd-Frank Act in the USA (2010), the Grenelle II Act in France (2010) or the Modern Slavery Act in the UK (2015). The second has to do with a kind of departure from the emphasis on similarities with financial reporting that characterised the initial developments of NFR by the GRI. The third aspect concerns the important role played by the financial sector and investors in this third wave, compared to the leading role played in the two previous waves by trade unions and civil society and their information needs. As Monciardini et al. (2020, p. 16) point out, the importance of investors is not surprising and "reflects the spirit of our times" given "four decades characterised by the financialisation of the global economy". Moreover, for these researchers, "investor-driven initiatives aimed at enhancing transparency and tackling climate issues and human rights violations could also be seen as a way to regain (or maintain) social legitimacy" (pp. 16–17).

Choudhury and Petrin (2019, p. 77) refer to NFR as being today inextricably linked to the "responsibility for public interest" currently attributed to corporations, i.e. CSR. According to these authors, governments are increasingly using the regulation of information disclosure as a tool to promote a plethora of public policy objectives, from reducing greenhouse gas emissions to promoting humanitarian aid. In addition to the traditional functions of reducing information asymmetry and promoting confidence in capital markets, information disclosure obligations have also come to focus on an additional function, that of the "promotion of social policy goals" (p. 78).

One concept that is important to present here in order to help the reader in grasping the current importance of NFR is that of "transparency". This is so because at the heart of an important part of the efforts of corporations and governments seems to be this concept. As acknowledged by Hess (2012, p. 52), "in policy debates centred around corporate accountability for social and environmental performance, transparency is always part of the discussion, if not the default approach."

In their literature review on transparency in organisations, Albu and Flyverbom (2019) identify two main streams of research, which are based on different conceptions of transparency. One of these streams focuses on the role of information, viewing transparency fundamentally as the sharing of information and its increase as depending only on the increase in the disclosure of information (p. 272). The other research stream relies on a concept of transparency that perceives it as a set of "complex communicative, organizational, and social processes rife with tensions and negotiations", largely calling into question the "assumed positive effects of information disclosure" (p. 277). In addition, the latter concept also "suggests that transparency projects may have unintended consequences and be a constitutive force in the recomposition of objects, subjects and relations" (ibid.).

Although considering the second stream of research on transparency more interesting from the point of view of understanding the phenomenon under discussion, the concept of transparency used in the book is that of the first stream of research mentioned. This is largely because this is a book that can be considered introductory and in which the various issues under examination are dealt with the depth allowed by the nature of the book, leaving room for in-depth study of such issues.

Transparency can undoubtedly be related to power, as it aims to "democratize information" and, by providing "access to and control over information and knowledge", gives power to those who do not have it (Mol, 2010, p. 135). The fact that information plays an increasingly important role in corporate governance and politics means that transparency plays an increasingly important role in the struggles to achieve objectives related to sustainable development and is no longer merely an invocation of the right-to-know (ibid.).

Choudhury (2016) stresses the importance of transparency and public corporate reporting from a social regulation point of view. In support, he uses recent examples at the time of writing. Thus, states Choudhury (2016, p. 185), when the UK government considered the number of women on company boards to be insufficient, rather than requiring corporations to increase that number, it required such organisations to disclose information about the number of women in management positions. Another example, offered by the same author, comes from the USA, where, to promote the reduction of violence in the Democratic Republic of Congo (DRC), "Congress directed the Securities and Exchange Commission to mandate corporate disclosure when using conflict minerals" (ibid.).

Choudhury and Petrin (2019, p. 85) go so far as to assert that "governments seem to turn first to disclosure requirements" as a way of dealing with such diverse issues as climate change, executive pay or diversity in the boards of directors. For these authors, it is a "meta-regulatory approach that focuses on regulating the process of regulation rather than regulating the issues directly", giving corporations "the flexibility to solve the problems they create" (p. 85). According to them, disclosure of information can be understood as "a weaker 'compromise' between the absence of any measures to regulate certain issues and direct regulatory measures" (ibid.).

Hess (2019, p. 7) lists four reasons why governments intensively use transparency policies in spite of the many doubts about their effects. A first reason is the assumption by many regulators that "information will lead to better decision making, and, therefore, even more information must lead to even better decision making" (ibid.). In this regard, Hess notes the frequent use of a quote by Justice Louis Brandeis, according to which "Sunlight is said to be the best of disinfectants". A second reason relates to the costs of transparency, which are usually supported by those responsible for the disclosure of the information and those who use it and not by the government. The third reason pertains to the attractiveness of this type of legislation for legislators of all political persuasions. The fourth reason is that passing this type of policies provides legislatures with "a sense of satisfaction" that actions to tackle the problem identified are being taken (ibid.). Hess concludes by asserting that "many view mandated disclosure as 'a kind of magical minimalism that delivers significant rewards at little cost'" (ibid.).

Whatever the case may be, as will be seen below, the problems related to the CSR issues in which this book focuses have been the object of regulatory policies based on the disclosure of information—on transparency. Several researchers have been discussing the role of transparency in mitigating problems pertaining to tax avoidance (Oats & Tuck, 2019) and corruption (Halter et al., 2009). At this point in the book, it is important to note that many other CSR-related problems were treated in a similar manner. Examples are climate change (Hahn et al., 2015), the aforementioned conflict minerals (Whitney, 2015), the so-called modern slavery (Ford & Nolan, 2020), inequality (Harvey et al., 2020), and corporate political activities (Favotto & Kollman, 2019), among many others.

Although acknowledging that "meaningful disclosures, particularly around governance and anti-corruption, are limited", Transparency International UK (2020, p. 7) asserts that "transparency is increasingly becoming a norm in the corporate world". According to this influential organisation, one can present a strong business case for corporate transparency. In a recent report in which it offers guidance on how corporations can enhance their transparency regarding a number of key anti-corruption risk areas, this organisation refers to four main ways in which transparency is likely to be advantageous to corporations (Transparency International UK, 2020). The first pertains to its assistance in securing and maintaining the trust of consumers, investors, and employees. The second has to do with an improved reputation, which transparency helps to obtain by showing that a corporation "has nothing to hide" (p. 17). Third, transparency ensures compliance. Fourth, it contributes to augmented competitive advantage. In Table 4.2, the main arguments offered by Transparency International UK are presented in a summary manner and in the form of a table.

Table 4.2 Outline of the business case for transparency

Main areas	Main arguments	
Trust	Consumer and customer trust	Consumers will pay more for products that promise total transparency
		Open and trusted companies are more likely to retain customers and have customers refer others to their services
	Investor trust	Transparency helps to build trust, which can help to attract and maintain investment
		Ensuring the quality of disclosure also helps to build investors' trust
	Employee trust	Transparency increases employee engagement
	Business-to-business trust	Transparency helps to foster business-to-business relationships
Reputation	In an increasingly interconnected world, having a well-respected brand is critical	
	Disclosure gives companies more control over brand and messaging	
Legislation	Corporate disclosure is increasingly becoming a legislative requirement. If nothing else, the potential financial and reputational damage of non-compliance should push companies towards disclosure.	
Competitive advantage	Transparent and ethical companies attract greater investment	
	Transparency is compatible with competitiveness	

Source: Based on Transparency International UK (2020, pp. 17–19)

References

Adams, C. A. (2020). Sustainability reporting and value creation. *Social and Environmental Accountability Journal, 40*(3), 191–197.

Albu, O. B., & Flyverbom, M. (2019). Organizational transparency: Conceptualizations, conditions, and consequences. *Business & Society, 58*(2), 268–297.

Alliance for Corporate Transparency. (2020). *Research report 2019: An analysis of the sustainability reports of 1000 companies pursuant to the EU non-financial reporting directive*. Alliance for Corporate Transparency.

Arvidsson, S. (2019). An exposé of the challenging practice development of sustainability reporting: From the first wave to the EU Directive (2014/95/EU). In S. Arvidsson (Ed.), *Challenges in managing sustainable business* (pp. 3–24). Palgrave McMillan.

Avi-Yonah, R. S. (2005). The cyclical transformations of the corporate form: A historical perspective on corporate social responsibility. *Delaware Journal of Corporate Law, 30*(3), 767–818.

Avi-Yonah, R. S. (2008). Corporate social responsibility and strategic tax behavior. In W. Schön (Ed.), *Tax and corporate governance* (pp. 183–198). Springer.

Avi-Yonah, R. S. (2014). Corporate taxation and corporate social responsibility. *New York University Journal of Law & Business, 11*(1), 1–29.

Batruch, C. (2017). Climate change and sustainability in the energy sector. *The Journal of World Energy Law & Business, 10*(5), 444–463.

Berger-Walliser, G., & Scott, I. (2018). Redefining corporate social responsibility in an era of globalization and regulatory hardening. *American Business Law Journal, 55*(1), 167–218.

Bommier, S., & Renouard, C. (2018). *L'Entreprise Comme Commun: Au-Delà de la RSE*. Éditions Charles Léopold Mayer.

Bommier, S., & Renouard, C. (2019*). Corporate responsibility in the climate crisis. Books and Ideas.* Accessed January 27, 2020, from https://booksandideas.net/Corporate-Responsibility-in-the-Climate-Crisis.html

Busco, C., Consolandi, C., Eccles, R. G., & Sofra, E. (2020). A preliminary analysis of SASB reporting: Disclosure topics, financial relevance, and the financial intensity of ESG materiality. *Journal of Applied Corporate Finance, 32*(2), 117–125.

Carroll, A. B. (1991). The pyramid of corporate social responsibility: Towards the moral management of organizational stakeholders. *Business Horizons, 34*(4), 39–48.

Chaffee, E. C. (2016). Collaboration theory: A theory of the charitable tax-exempt nonprofit corporation. *UC Davis Law Review, 49*(5), 1719–1781.

Chaffee, E. C. (2017). The origins of corporate social responsibility. *University of Cincinnati Law Review, 85*, 353–373.

Chaffee, E. C. (2019). Collaboration theory and corporate tax avoidance. *Washington & Lee Law Review, 76*, 93–162.

Chaffee, E. C. (2020). A theory of the business trust. *University of Cincinnati Law Review, 88*(3), 797–842.

Choudhury, B. (2016). Social disclosure. *Berkeley Business Law Journal, 13*, 183–216.

Choudhury, B., & Petrin, M. (2019). *Corporate duties to the public*. Cambridge University Press.

Crane, A., Matten, D., Glozer, S., & Spence, L. (2019). *Business ethics: Managing corporate citizenship and sustainability in the age of globalization*. Oxford: Oxford University Press.

DNV GL/UNGC (United Nations Global Compact). (2020). *Uniting business in the decade of action: Building on 20 years of progress*. DNV GL/UNGC.

European Commission. (2001). *Green paper – Promoting a European framework for Corporate Social Responsibility*. COM(2001). 366 final.

European Commission. (2002). *Corporate social responsibility: A business contribution to sustainable development*. COM(2002). 347 final.

European Commission. (2006). *Communication from the Commission to the European Parliament, the Council and the European Economic and Social Committee: Implementing the partnership for growth and jobs: Making Europe a Pole of excellence on corporate social responsibility*. COM (2006) 136 final.

European Commission. (2011). *Communication from the Commission to the European Parliament, the Council, the European Economic and Social Committee and the Committee of the Regions. A renewed EU strategy 2011–14 for Corporate Social Responsibility*. COM 2011(681) final.

European Commission. (2017). Communication from the commission — Guidelines on non-financial reporting (methodology for reporting non-financial information). 2017/C 215/01. *Official Journal of the European Union*.

European Union. (2014). Directive 2014/95/EU of the European Parliament and of the Council of 22 October 2014 amending Directive 2013/34/EU as regards disclosure of non-financial and diversity information by certain large undertakings and groups. *Official Journal of the European Union*.

Favotto, A., & Kollman, K. (2019). Mixing business with politics: Does corporate social responsibility end where lobbying transparency begins? *Regulation & Governance*. https://doi.org/10.1111/rego.12275

Ford, J., & Nolan, J. (2020). Regulating transparency on human rights and modern slavery in corporate supply chains: The discrepancy between human rights due diligence and the social audit. *Australian Journal of Human Rights, 26*(1), 27–45.

Freeman, R. E. (1994). The politics of stakeholder theory: Some future directions. *Business Ethics Quarterly, 4*(4), 409–421.

Geva, A. (2008). Three models of corporate social responsibility: Interrelationships between theory, research, and practice. *Business and Society Review, 113*(1), 1–41.

Gray, R. (2010). Is accounting for sustainability actually accounting for sustainability… and how would we know? An exploration of narratives of organisations and the planet. *Accounting, Organizations and Society, 35*(1), 47–62.

GRI. (2020). *Consolidated set of GRI sustainability reporting standards 2020*. GRI.

Hahn, R., Reimsbach, D., & Schiemann, F. (2015). Organizations, climate change, and transparency: Reviewing the literature on carbon disclosure. *Organization & Environment, 28*(1), 80–102.

Halter, M., Arruda, M., & Halter, R. (2009). Transparency to reduce corruption? *Journal of Business Ethics, 84*, 373–385.

Harris, J. D., & Freeman, R. E. (2008). The impossibility of the separation thesis: A response to Joakim Sandberg. *Business Ethics Quarterly, 18*(4), 541–548.

Harvey, C., Maclean, M., & Price, M. (2020). Executive remuneration and the limits of disclosure as an instrument of corporate governance. *Critical Perspectives on Accounting, 69*, 102089.

Heal, G. (2008). *When principles pay: Corporate social responsibility and the bottom line*. New York: Columbia University Press.

Hess, D. (2012). Combating corruption through corporate transparency: Using enforcement discretion to improve disclosure. *Minnesota Journal of International Law, 21*, 42–70.

Hess, D. (2019). The transparency trap: Non-financial disclosure and the responsibility of business to respect human rights. *American Business Law Journal, 56*(1), 5–53.

Holme, R., & Watts, P. (2000). *Corporate social responsibility: Making good business sense*. World Business Council for Sustainable Development.

Hopkins, M. (2007). *Corporate social responsibility and international development: Is business the solution*. Earthscan.

IIRC. (2021). *The international framework*. IIRC.

Kinderman, D. (2018). Global and EU-level corporate social responsibility: Dynamism, growth, and conflict. In M. In Kunze & S. Nährlich (Eds.), *Gesellschaftliche Verantwortung von Unternehmen in Deutschland* (pp. 101–113). Springer.

KPMG. (2005). *KPMG international survey of corporate responsibility reporting 2005*. KPMG.

KPMG. (2017). *KPMG international survey of corporate responsibility reporting 2017*. KPMG.

KPMG. (2020). *KPMG international survey of sustainability reporting 2020*. KPMG.

Landrum, N. E. (2014). Defining a base of the pyramid strategy. *International Journal of Business and Emerging Markets, 6*(4), 286–297.

Lin-Hi, N. (2010). The problem with a narrow-minded interpretation of CSR. Why CSR has nothing to do with philanthropy. *Ramon Llull Journal of Applied Ethics, 1*(1), 75–95.

Matten, D., & Moon, J. (2004). Corporate social responsibility education in Europe. *Journal of Business Ethics, 54*, 323–337.

Meuer, J., Koelbel, J., & Hoffmann, V. H. (2020). On the nature of corporate sustainability. *Organization & Environment, 33*(3), 319–341.

Mol, A. P. J. (2010). The future of transparency: Power, pitfalls and promises. *Global Environmental Politics, 10*, 133–143.

Monciardini, D., Mähönen, J. T., & Tsagas, G. (2020). Rethinking non-financial reporting: A blueprint for structural regulatory changes. *Accounting, Economics, and Law: A Convivium, 10* (2), 20200092.

Oats, L., & Tuck, P. (2019). Corporate tax avoidance: Is tax transparency the solution? *Accounting and Business Research, 49*(5), 565–583.

Orbie, J., & Babarinde, O. (2008). The social dimension of globalization and EU development policy: Promoting core labour standards and corporate social responsibility. *Journal of European Integration, 30*(3), 459–477.

Rasche, A., Morsing, M., & Moon, J. (2017). The changing role of business in global society: CSR and beyond. In A. Rasche, M. Morsing, & J. Moon (Eds.), *Corporate social responsibility: Strategy, communication, governance* (pp. 1–30). Cambridge University Press.

Renouard, C. (2012). The private sector and the fight against poverty. *Field Actions Science Reports, Special Issue, 4*, 62–67.

Renouard, C. (2015). *Éthique et Entreprise*. Éditions de l'Atelier.

Renouard, C., & Ezvan, C. (2018). Corporate social responsibility towards human development: A capabilities framework. *Business Ethics: A European Review, 27*(2), 144–155.

Schwartz, M. S., & Carroll, A. B. (2003). Corporate social responsibility: A three domain approach. *Business Ethics Quarterly, 13*, 503–530.

Sethi, S. P., Rovenpor, J. L., & Demir, M. (2017). Enhancing the quality of reporting in corporate social responsibility guidance documents: The roles of ISO 26000, global reporting initiative and CSR-sustainability monitor. *Business and Society Review, 122*(2), 139–163.

Stolowy, H., & Paugam, L. (2018). The expansion of non-financial reporting: An exploratory study. *Accounting and Business Research, 48*(5), 525–548.

Tarquinio, L., & Posadas, S. C. (2020). Exploring the term "non-financial information": An academics' view. *Meditari Accountancy Research, 28*(5), 727–749.

Transparency International UK. (2020). *Open business: Principles and guidance for anti-corruption corporate transparency*. Transparency International UK.

Tsagas, G., & Villiers, C. (2020). Why "less is more" in non-financial reporting initiatives: Concrete steps towards supporting sustainability. *Accounting, Economics, and Law: A Convivium, 10*(2), 20180045.

UNGC (2008). *Corporate citizenship in the world economy: UNGC*. UNGC.

Visser, W. (2006). Revisiting Carroll's CSR pyramid: An African perspective. In M. Huniche & E. R. Pedersen (Eds.), *Corporate citizenship in developing countries: New partnership perspectives* (pp. 29–56). Copenhagen Business School Press.

Visser, W. (2008). Corporate social responsibility in developing countries. In A. Crane, A. McWilliams, D. Matten, J. Moon, & D. S. Siegel (Eds.), *The Oxford handbook of corporate social responsibility* (pp. 473–499). Oxford University Press.

Visser, W. (2014). *CSR 2.0: Transforming corporate sustainability and responsibility*. Springer.

WEF. (2020). *Measuring stakeholder capitalism – Towards common metrics and consistent reporting of sustainable value creation*. WEF.

Whitney, T. (2015). Conflict minerals, black markets, and transparency: The legislative background of Dodd-Frank Section 1502 and its historical lessons. *Journal of Human Rights, 14*(2), 183–200.

Zinenko, A., Rovira, M. R., & Montiel, I. (2015). The fit of the social responsibility standard ISO 26000 within other CSR instruments: Redundant or complementary? *Sustainability Accounting, Management and Policy Journal, 6*(4), 498–526.

Part II
The Fight Against Corruption and Tax Behaviour as Corporate Social Responsibility Issues

Chapter 5
The Fight Against Corruption

Abstract In this chapter the role of CSR in the fight against corruption is explored. Discussions on corruption and its effects, especially the negative ones on societies and corporations, as well as on how the CSR-related instruments presented in the previous chapter may help in the fight against corruption, are offered. The fight against corruption is analysed as a CSR issue and is presented as an integral part of any corporation's social responsibility. The issue of how some CSR-related instruments deal with the fight against corruption is addressed. The importance of anti-corruption CSR policies and the reporting thereof is outlined as a basis for an effective fight against corruption and associated phenomena.

Keywords Anti-corruption reporting · Corporate social responsibility · CSR-related instruments · Fight against corruption

5.1 Some Problems Pertaining to the Definition and Measurement of Corruption

5.1.1 Definition

Within the social sciences, especially in the case of economics, most of the studies on the phenomenon of corruption have restricted the examination to public sector corruption (Hodgson, 2013). For example, for a long period, the World Bank adopted a definition of corruption as the "abuse of public power for private benefit" (Tanzi, 1998). Many studies examine corruption as a phenomenon that takes place between, on the one side, public officials and, on the other side, actors from the private sector. Such a focus does not allow us to depict the real role of the business sector in this phenomenon.

Hodgson (2013, p. 157) puts forward a possible reason for such a focus on the public sector when studying corruption, that of the "widespread influence of pro-market, antistate, libertarian ideology". From such a perspective, curbing corruption is tantamount to reducing the size of the state, which is seen as the solution to

M. Castelo Branco, *Corporate Social Responsibility, the Fight Against Corruption and Tax Behaviour*, CSR, Sustainability, Ethics & Governance,
https://doi.org/10.1007/978-3-662-63735-7_5

the problem at hand (ibid.). Most of the authors who share this view are not nearly as concerned with the abuse of power by corporate managers as they are with the abuse of power by public officials (ibid.).

Defining corruption merely as the abuse of public power for private benefit raises many reasons. Probably the most relevant one pertains to the fact that the corruption taking place solely within the private sector gets ignored (Habib & Zurawicki, 2001). There are a plethora of studies analysing corruption within the private sector (e.g., Aguilera & Abhijeet, 2008; Argandoña, 2003, 2005; Castro et al., 2020; Dion, 2010; Gopinath, 2008; Halter et al., 2009; O'Hara, 2014).

To deal with this problem, Rodriguez et al. (2006) suggest the replacement of the term "public power" by "authority", thus allowing the consideration of corruption occurring strictly between private parties. This is what the United States Agency for International Development (USAID) has done (USAID, 2005). Others have replaced the term "public power" with "entrusted power". One prominent example of such a solution adopted is Jeremy Pope, former head of Transparency International (TI). Pope offers a definition of corruption as "the misuse of entrusted power for private benefit" (Pope, 2000, p. 22). Following Pope, this phenomenon has been defined by TI in pretty much the same way as "the abuse of entrusted power for private gain" (Errath et al., 2005, p. 7). Corruption is defined in a similar manner in ISO 26000, in which there is an explicit acknowledgement that it not only includes bribery (soliciting, offering or accepting a bribe) of or by public officials but also bribery in the private sector (as well as conflict of interest, fraud, money laundering and trading in influence) (ISO, 2010, 2017).

These definitions allow to explicitly consider corruption arising exclusively within the private sector. Pope (2000, p. 139) recognised the spread of such "private-to-private corruption". Private-to-private corruption occurs in traditional areas such as distributorships, procurement, proprietary technical and commercial data, retail display space, scrap disposal (Pope, 2000), but also in areas such as gambling, safety tests on products, or loan procurement (Castro et al., 2020). Hence, corruption is a phenomenon regarding which one has to acknowledge the central role of corporations in all circumstances. They play such a role both when corruption occurs completely within the business sector but also in cases in which there is the involvement of public officials. In these latter cases, corporations may be said to represent the other side of the "demand side" agents of corruption, that is, of those who practice corruption (Palan et al., 2010, p. 180).

To understand the role of the private sector in combating corruption, one needs to understand its role in creating such a phenomenon. This is not a passive role. To get an idea of the role played by large corporations, one need only look at the OECD (2014) report on cross-border bribery, which presents evidence from the examination of 427 cases of bribery recorded since 1999. This report reveals that most of these cases are the responsibility of large corporations, and their leadership is involved or at least aware of the actions, debunking the myth of the "rogue employee", as the report itself states.

Hodgson (2013, p. 159) argues that "the idea that corruption *always* involves 'private gain' is almost as problematic" as offering a definition of corruption as always involving the public sector. As an example of "bribing for higher motives", Hodgson (2013, p. 160) offers the case of the payments to Nazi officials by Oskar Schindler in an attempt of preventing the incarceration in concentration camps of over a thousand Jews. Hodgson refers to the objection associated with the fact that the motives behind corruption are most commonly associated with personal gain, purportedly justifying the retention of the term "private gain" in the definition, as confusing definition with description. One also has to acknowledge that there are instances in which what motivates the engagement in corruption is gaining organisational advantage rather than personal gain (Castro et al., 2020). Acknowledging these problems, and focusing on corporate corruption, Castro et al. (2020, p. 938) propose defining it as "the misuse of formal power by a corporate representative for personal and/or organizational benefit".

Rabl and Kühlmann (2009, p. 3) proposed a more complex definition of corruption that seems to address adequately the problems presented above. They define corruption as:

> deviant behavior which manifests itself in an abuse of a function in politics, society, or economy in favor of another person or institution. This abuse of a function occurs on one's own or the other's initiative in order to achieve an advantage for oneself or a third party. As a result, a damage or disadvantage to politics, society, or economy is expected or does actually appear. The corrupt actions are kept secret in mutual, amicable agreement.

Another equally interesting definition that has the merit (at least for me) of explicitly considering corruption as unethical behaviour and as detrimental to the common good is that of O'Hara (2014). According to O'Hara, corruption is "a form of unethical behavior and wrongdoing which is the outcome of abuse of power for an individual's or group's benefit against the common good" (p. 293).

However, besides the two problems presented above, that seem to have been resolved by these two definitions, the definition of corruption as the abuse of public power for private benefit presents the additional problem of depicting corruption as a one-way process driven by greed of corrupt officials (UNDP, 2008, p. 18). The anti-state and libertarian perspective characteristic of many economics and management scholars mentioned above also allows us to explain this bias. Almost all corruption acts happen between two players, and it may not be the case that power is on the side of the corrupt player to whom power has been entrusted (ibid.).

Whatever the case may be, corruption is usually understood as assuming numerous forms. Menocal et al. (2015, p. 12) outline the most common categories of corruption in the form of a table (Table 5.1).

I must also ask the reader to have in mind Fleming and Zyglidopoulos's (2009) approach to corporate corruption as blending corruption as defined above and corporate crime, this latter being defined as "activities in which the corporation as a whole benefits from the illegality, rather than specific individuals in the firm" (p. 6). This take on corporate corruption leads to include in it activities such as anti-competitive behaviour, illegal environmental damage, irresponsible working conditions, marketing and sale of unsafe products, or tax evasion, as mentioned in the introduction to this book. This idea stems from a view of corporate corruption as

Table 5.1 Most common categories of corruption

Categories of corruption	Description
Bribery	The act of dishonestly persuading someone to act in one's favour by a payment or other inducement. Inducements can take the form of gifts, loans, fees, rewards or other advantages (taxes, services, donations, etc.). The use of bribes can lead to collusion (e.g. inspectors under-reporting offences in exchange for bribes) and/or extortion (e.g. bribes extracted against the threat of over-reporting)
Embezzlement	To steal, misdirect or misappropriate funds or assets placed in one's trust or under one's control. From a legal point of view, embezzlement need not necessarily be or involve corruption
Facilitation payment	A small payment, also called a "speed" or "grease" payment, made to secure or expedite the performance of a routine or necessary action to which the payer has legal or other entitlement
Fraud	The act of intentionally and dishonestly deceiving someone in order to gain an unfair or illegal advantage (financial, political or otherwise)
Collusion	An arrangement between two or more parties designed to achieve an improper purpose, including influencing improperly the actions of another party
Extortion	The act of impairing or harming, or threatening to impair or harm, directly or indirectly, any party or the property of the party to influence improperly the actions of a party
Patronage, clientelism and nepotism	Patronage at its core means the support given by a patron. In government, it refers to the practice of appointing people directly

Source: Menocal et al. (2015, p. 12)

encompassing not only situations in which the individuals in the organisation benefit but also situations resulting in benefits for the whole organisation (ibid.). I believe one can expand further this view to consider activities that do not conform to the definition of corporate crime but are beneficial (actually or potentially) to the corporation while being detrimental to society as a whole, such as lobbying or the funding of political parties (in the countries in which they are permitted).

Regarding the distinction between lobbying and corruption, Fjeldstad et al. (2017, p. 72) note that the two words are basically synonymous to citizens in many countries. This happens in a great measure because the basic goal is the same, that of influencing government decisions. As these researchers put it, notwithstanding the differences between the two phenomena (including that of lobbying being legal and legitimate, whereas the case is not the same with corruption), "lobbying and some forms of corruption have something important in common; both are ways of obtaining help from the public sector in exchange for something" (ibid.).

Although I will not explicitly use the approach of conflating corruption and lobbying in what follows and focus on the common forms of corruption presented above, activities that can be included in the expanded definition of corruption will be taken into account, albeit not in such a detailed manner as the ones usually considered as corruption. This will be done for several reasons. The first has to do with what was asserted above regarding lobbying and political contributions. The second concerns the fact that some of the most influential CSR voluntary initiatives, such as the OECD Guidelines for MNEs, explicitly include political contributions as an aspect of the fight against corruption (OECD, 2011, p. 48). The UNGC, in its Guide for Anti-Corruption Risk Assessment, referring to the manyfold forms of corruption, considers political donations as a form of bribery and mentions the "movement of high-level employees from public sector jobs to private sector jobs and vice versa", the so-called revolving door phenomenon, as a form of corruption (UNGC, 2013, pp. 12–13) explicitly.

5.1.2 Measurement

Unlike many other phenomena associated with CSR, it is almost impossible to obtain hard evidence of actions of corruption. Regarding phenomena such as child labour or environmental pollution, the obtention of evidence such as photographs or descriptions by third parties is not nearly as difficult as in the case of corruption (Hills et al., 2009). As emphasised by Fisman and Miguel (2008, p. 18), actions of corruption take place "out of sight" and the obtention of an "obvious paper trail of what took place" is almost impossible if the parties involved in it are doing "a halfway decent job of it". Hence, most measures of corruption are based on perceptions of corruption, either of political experts, people conducting business in the country, or even ordinary people (IMF, 2019; Graycar, 2015).

If we take the best-known indirect measure of country-level corruption, the TI's Corruption Perceptions Index (CPI), we realise that it is fraught with difficulties of interpretation. The CPI is a composite indicator, i.e. compiled from various sources, all of which are based on agents' perception of the level of corruption in the public sector in a given country. This index is expressed in the form of a ranking, using a score to express the position of countries in it. There has been much criticism of this way of measuring corruption, and many shortcomings have been pointed out. A key point, which must be taken into account when analysing the evolution over time of a country's position in the CPI, is that such a position is only relative, meaning that the fact that a country rises on the list of countries implies that a certain number of countries will fall on that same list, regardless of what has happened in terms of the empirical phenomenon to which it refers. Another crucial aspect to be considered is that the CPI is an index based on perceptions regarding the reality of corruption, and this raises some questions to be taken into consideration when analysing it. First of all, it is important to recognise that the views of the same person on the empirical phenomenon of corruption will almost certainly be different at different points in time, even if the underlying empirical reality has not changed. Therefore, even if the agents whose opinions are used to build the CPI are the same in different years, which is not the case, comparisons over time should be made with great caution. In addition, the fact that the methodology itself varies from year to year and from country to country means that comparisons over time with respect to one country and comparisons between countries should be made and analysed with extreme care. With respect to cross-country comparability, it is important to note that the sources used are often different.

There are other frailties regarding both the definition of corruption and its measurement that one must acknowledge. However interesting O'Hara's (2014) or Rabl and Kühlmann's (2009) definitions of corruption may be, there are still some aspects that surely remain to be addressed. One of such aspects, that of offering and facilitating opportunities for corruption, which some call the "supply-side of corruption" (Christensen, 2011; Palan et al., 2010), is especially relevant for the issues on which this book focuses, namely that of tax behaviour, as well as for making some commentaries regarding some measurements of country-level corruption. This supply side of corruption remains hidden in the definitions mentioned above, and this implies that the measurements of corruption based on such definitions do not take into account this other side of corruption.

Besides the difficulties mentioned above, the CPI does not consider at all how the different countries position themselves in terms of the supply side of corruption. This is why countries like Switzerland or the Netherlands appear very well ranked in the CPI despite their important role in facilitating and promoting corruption. It is well known that Switzerland (and other countries with similar characteristics) facilitates and promotes tax avoidance and tax evasion, money laundering, corruption, among others, contributing substantially to the existence of these types of practices (Christensen, 2011; Palan et al., 2010). Therefore, one can express some surprise that among the countries considered to be among the least corrupt according to the CPI, there are countries where much of the revenue from corruption and associated phenomena is deposited, such as Switzerland. In the most recent CPI, that of 2020, Singapore, Switzerland, the Netherlands, and Luxembourg appear among with a rank below 10.

In October 2019, Transparency International UK (2019) published a report with the illuminating title "At your service—Investigating how UK businesses and institutions help corrupt individuals and regimes launder their money and reputations". With reference to the damages caused by corruption, including the loss of funds that could be used to properly fund basic services such as health or education, the authors of this report acknowledge that, although it seems to many to be an essentially foreign problem, there is no escaping the fact that UK-based services often facilitate this type of phenomenon and are the destination of the associated revenues. The study presented in this report used data from the analysis of over 400 cases in which UK organisations have been involved in providing services that have facilitated the laundering of money obtained from corruption. The amount of money involved was at least £325 billion. There were 116 countries where the cases made it possible to obtain this amount unduly. This report suggests that many of the major cases of bribery, embezzlement and manipulated public procurement seem to be linked to a UK-based connection: a secret company in the British Virgin Islands, a mansion in the London Borough of Mayfair, a British bank.

Hence, instruments such as the CPI cannot account for the reality of corruption in all its complexity. If they did, a substantial part of its usefulness might be lost. Their use should be complemented by other available instruments, which provide an idea of how well countries rank in terms of their contribution to the supply side of corruption. One of such instruments is the Tax Justice Network's Financial Secrecy Index, according to which, in its 2020 edition, the eight first places are occupied by the Cayman Islands, the USA, Switzerland, Hong Kong, Singapore, Luxembourg, Japan, and the Netherlands.

5.2 Why Corruption Matters?

Corruption is viewed as a major obstacle to sustainable development, both by academics (Aidt, 2011, 2016; López Claros, 2015, 2017; Mugellini & Villeneuve, 2019) and by international organisations (United Nations, 2019). One can only express surprise for the issue of corruption not having been included in the eight areas of intervention covered by the 2000 Millennium Development Goals. Notwithstanding, this issue has been given some importance in the 2030 Agenda for Sustainable Development and the Sustainable Development Goals (SDGs). SDG 16 (Promote peaceful and inclusive societies for sustainable development, provide access to justice for all and build effective, accountable and inclusive institutions at all levels) includes target 16.5, which makes explicit reference to the purpose of substantially reduce corruption and bribery in all its forms. In addition, targets 16.6 and 16.7 can be seen as inextricably linked with corruption. These targets focus on the development of effective, accountable and transparent institutions at all levels (target 16.6) and ensuring responsive, inclusive, participatory, and representative decision-making at all levels (target 16.7).

The United Nations's (2019) "World Public Sector Report 2019" focuses on the SDG 16. In this document, the inclusion of SDG 16 on par with goals on issues such as those pertaining to education, health, or poverty, is considered as a "game changer" (p. 2). In it, corruption is acknowledged as a phenomenon hindering the achievement of the entire set of SDGs, and the fight against corruption is viewed as underpinning all efforts to achieve such a set of goals (p. 40). This United Nations document offers some relevant estimates in support of such view: the costs associated with corruption amount to at least 5% of the global gross domestic product (GDP); about US$1 trillion is paid in bribes each year; 25% of the GDP of African states is lost to corruption every year; 20–40% of official development assistance is also lost to corruption every year. Besides these numbers, the World Public Sector Report 2019 also includes some estimates pertaining to impacts in sectors such as health and water and refers to the gruesome estimate of about 14,000 children dying every year as an indirect consequence of corruption.

In his attempt at answering the question "how does corruption destroy prosperity?", López Claros (2017, p. 34) is adamant in asserting that "corruption damages the social and institutional fabric of a country by undermining sustainable economic development, cutting into government revenue, and limiting productivity". López Claros (2015, 2017) adduces several reasons why corruption has such a detrimental effect. I will refer only to some of them, expounding the arguments of this eminent economist.

First, corruption leads citizens to question whether taxes really amount to a public benefit, and this makes them feel justified in engaging in not paying their fair share or even in engaging in acts of corruption themselves. In this way, the capacity of the government to collect revenue to fund its activities is reduced, and this restrains its ability to finance adequately such important activities as health and education. This argument is especially relevant for this book, given the link it establishes between corruption and taxation.

Second, corruption leads to distortions in public investment. As large capital projects that represent opportunities for corruption are more tempting as a way of collecting bribes, expenditures on areas such as health and education are reduced. In this connection, López Claros (2015, p. 16) refers to the distortion of incentives that in developed countries is linked to the "multi-billion-dollar industry" that is the lobbying industry. This economist goes as far as asserting that the reality of lobbying "is often one where corporate cash greatly degrades the ability of the political system to address real problems" (ibid.). This reality is in opposition to one of lobbying fulfilling a "beneficial public purpose" as it would if it were "limited to enlightened public discourse on the merits of proposed pieces of legislation—through which interested parties, in a spirit of consultation, aim to help legislators better understand the full ramifications of different courses of action" (ibid.).

Third, corruption undermines the development of the private sector, as it discourages investment and innovation and encourages inefficiency. Related to this, López Claros considers that corruption also contributes to a misallocation of human resources. As put by López Claros (2017, p. 35), "to sustain a system of corruption, officials and those who pay them are constrained to invest time and effort to developing certain skills, nurturing relationships, and creating supporting institutions and opaque systems, such as secret bank accounts and off-the-books transactions".

Fourth, there is evidence of a positive relationship between the levels of corruption and of the shadow economy, as well as the detrimental effect of corruption on foreign direct investment (FDI). As argued by López Claros (2015, p. 14), "because it acts in ways that are indistinguishable from a tax; other things being equal, investors will always prefer to establish themselves in less corrupt countries".

Fifth, corruption is related to worsened income distribution and inequality, reduced social spending, unequal access to education, and the use of their wealth by the wealthy and powerful to lobby for policies that are favourable to them at the detriment of society. In connection with this, López Claros (2017, p. 17) explicitly refers to the distortions to the tax system related to the ability of the "wealthy and powerful" of using their political connections to make sure that such a system is beneficial to them.

Sixth, "because corruption is a betrayal of trust, it diminishes the legitimacy of the state and the moral stature of the bureaucracy in the eyes of the population" (López Claros, 2015, p. 18). Related to this, albeit López Claros does not refer to it, one

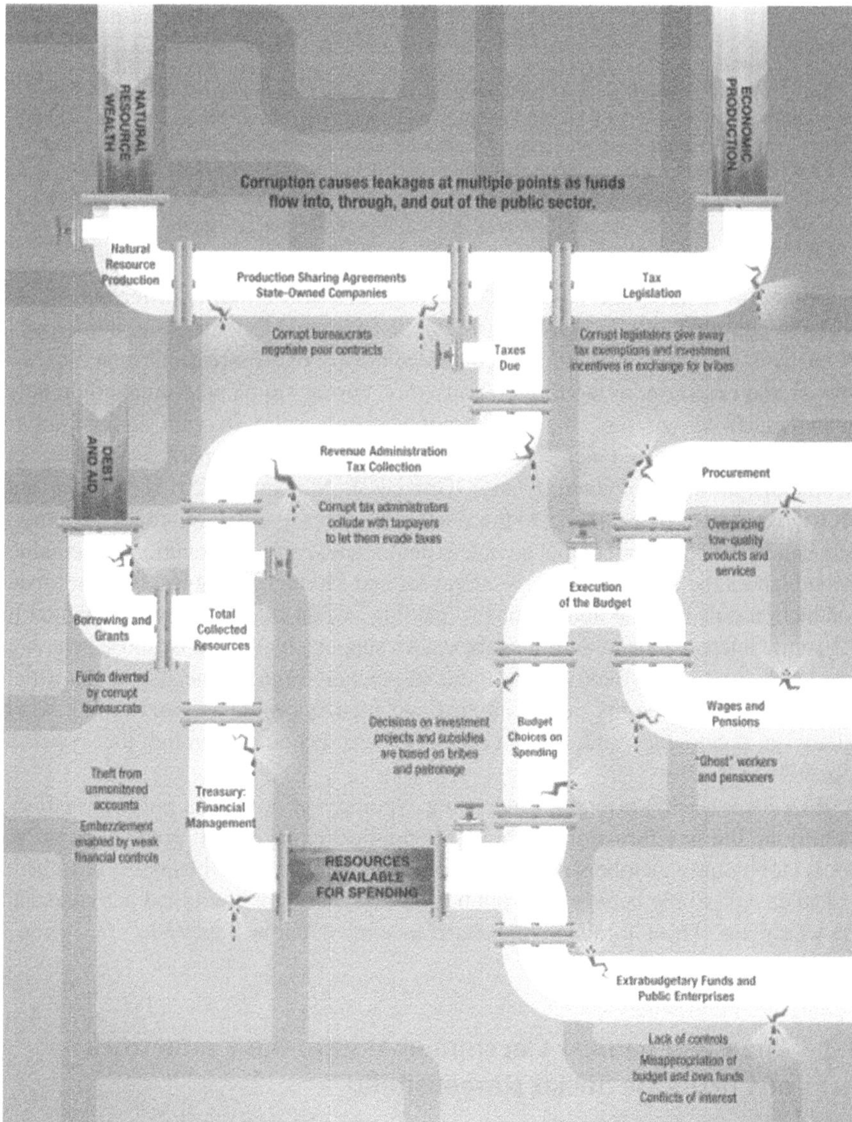

Fig. 5.1 Corruption leakages in the public sector. Source: IMF (2019, p. 42)

should refer to the detrimental effects of corruption on the legitimacy of the market economy (Tanzi, 1998) and perhaps also of democracy (Tanzi, 1998; USAID, 2005).

Offering a more detailed view of how corruption affects the public sector financially, the IMF (2019, p. 42) provides a picture (reproduced in Fig. 5.1) illustrating the manifold leakages of funds occurring in the public sector as a consequence of corruption.

This first part of the discussion on why corruption matters can be summarised as follows:

> Thus, from a public perspective, corruption can contribute to political instability, undermine economic growth, hinder FDI, undermine public trust, shift resources away from public services, and compromise entrepreneurship, competition, and welfare determinants. Moreover, it can undermine economic development, defined either narrowly or broadly as sustainable development. Even where it produces short-run efficiencies, corruption has a tendency to cancel out these efficiencies in the long run. Overall, corruption is therefore a detriment to public interests. (Choudhury & Petrin, 2019, p. 283)

Be that as it may, one has to acknowledge that corruption is different and has different consequences in rich countries when compared to their poor counterparts. Whereas in the latter, corruption seems to be mostly of a more direct type, such as bribery and extortion, in the former, corruption appears to be predominantly related to the manifold ways of the gaming of society's rules to gain some kind of illegitimate advantage (such as lobbying, funding political parties and election campaigns, conflicts of interest, etc.) (Graycar & Monaghan, 2015). Graycar and Monaghan (2015, p. 591) refer to these latter practices as existing "in the penumbra between legitimate conduct that advances democratic capitalist function and conduct that advances the interests of a few". Graycar and Monaghan suggest that legitimate conduct crosses the line and becomes "gaming" when they become detrimental to the public interest and "undermines the values supposedly upheld by those behaving improperly" (ibid.). Moreover, as these researchers argue, "the degree to which legitimate conduct harms public interest and trust is central in determining when otherwise acceptable (and often necessary) acts become 'gaming the system'" (pp. 591–592).

Wilkinson (2015) offers an interesting typology of corporate political activity, identifying the five forms of corporation's political engagement: political contributions; lobbying; memberships of trade associations and business chambers; exchanges of people between the public and private sectors; political activities and the workplace. These forms are presented in some detail in Table 5.2.

5.3 The Fight against Corruption Within the Framework of Corporate Social Responsibility

5.3.1 Arguments for CSR Anti-corruption

From a CSR perspective, the fight against corruption can be viewed from two different perspectives. One is the ethical perspective or "ethical case" (Brew et al., 2011), according to which "corruption is also (and especially) an ethical problem" (Argandoña, 2007, p. 482). The agent who acts "against the duties of his position" is acting in such a manner that is "unjust to his principal and is not fulfilling the duties that correspond to his position" (ibid.). What is more, and this is the most important aspect for me, given that I see CSR as the contribution of corporations to sustainable

Table 5.2 Forms of corporate political engagement

Activity	Description
Political donations and expenditure	Contributions made directly or indirectly to a political party or its local branches, elected officials or political candidates Contributions made to an organisation or activity aligned with a political cause such as a research organisation or think tank, assisting with the drafting of legislation, carrying our funding or research
Lobbying	Formal advocacy carried out by in-house lobbyists, consultant lobbyists and trade associations Informal advocacy by board members, senior executives or specialists Lobbying activities can include meetings, position papers, communications, administration, research, drafting proposals for legislation and providing staff resources and meeting rooms for political committees, such as UK all-party parliamentary groups Indirect lobbying can include building supporting constituencies and initiating and funding community campaigns (so-called astro-turfing) by engaging and mobilising organisations such as research institutes, charities and action groups and initiating, funding and managing social media campaigns
Trade associations and business chambers	Memberships of trade associations and business chambers that lobby on behalf of their members
Exchanges of people between business and the public sector	Revolving door: Post-employment positions, two-way, to and from public office Secondment: Long-term and short-term work experience placements in either direction Associated politicians: Depending on the laws of the jurisdiction, elected politicians may be contracted as consultants to the company or appointed to the board
Political activities and the workplace	Release for public office, such as carrying out duties as a local councillor Unpaid leave to campaign for office

Source: Wilkinson (2015, p. 11)

human development and take into account the plethora of negative effects described above, often this unfairness has detrimental impacts also in other agents (ibid.). This is the view to which I adhere.

Notwithstanding, I should note that some authors, such as Linder and Linder (2008), are able to offer some kind of ethical justification for actions of corruption. These researchers consider that moral problems may not be present in all situations, offering as an example of such situations the cases where corruption may be thought of as a competitive requirement. For example, in countries where corruption is a widespread phenomenon, and no penalty is imposed, corporations should act in accordance with prevailing conventions.

The other perspective is the "managerial standpoint" (Sampson, 2019) or the "business case" (Brew et al., 2011). Sampson (2019, p. 284) argues that from the corporation's standpoint, the fight against corruption need not be an ethical problem. As put by Sampson, "there is a practical side: acting corrupt may be bad for business" (ibid.). The eventual benefits of corruption, such as those derived from the possibility of corruption allowing "to overcome certain bureaucratic barriers" (the 'lubrication' thesis, via speed payments)", are confronted with the risks associated with it, whether they are of financial, legal or reputational nature (ibid). From this standpoint, "promoting anti-corruption may actually be good business" (ibid.). According to this perspective, "one of the most compelling reasons for companies to review their ethical behavior is likely to be that of self-interest" (Pope, 2000, p. 144).

According to Hills et al. (2009), managers of corporations operating in developing countries have always been concerned about reputational risks from corruption. There are other additional benefits derived from promoting the fight against corruption. These are associated with other costs and risks besides the reputational ones that managers of corporations are becoming more and more aware of, namely financial costs and legal risks (Hills et al., 2009). The consequences of engaging in corrupt actions include large fines and disqualification from future government procurement (ibid.). Some estimates of the cost of bribery and corruption suggest that every year, losses associated with corruption amount to over 5% of global GDP and bribes amount to over US$1 trillion (Mooney et al., 2016). For Mooney et al. (2016, p. 5), besides being deleterious to governments and society, the cost of corruption "can be brought to bear on companies and their investors". According to other estimates, corruption may imply an increase of about 10% to the cost of doing business globally and 25% to the cost of procurement contracts in developing countries (ibid.). The costs associated with corporate corruption scandals, such as those presented in Table 5.3, are staggering.

Besides financial costs, legal risks, and reputational risks, Brew et al. (2011, pp. 5–7) refer to the following aspects: "known as clean" and repeat demands; blackmail, no recourse and security risks; erosion of internal trust and confidence; and corporations' vested interest in sustainable development. To these aspects, Pope (2000) adds another relevant risk to corporations, the one in which they are placing themselves in when corruption abroad by their employees is tolerated, given that it may be only a matter of time for them to be the victims of corrupt actions on the part of these latter organisational members.

One important argument for corporations' engagement with the fight against corruption that is in some way linked with the self-interest perspective has been put forward by Rose-Ackerman (2002). According to this prominent researcher, given that they benefit from the market system and that the normative justification of markets is based on their efficiency, corporations have an obligation to act in such ways as to improve the efficient functioning markets. Moreover, the success of corporations relies as much on the existence of a market system that functions smoothly as on a state that facilitates market activity and maintains order and stability (ibid.).

Table 5.3 Reported losses from some corporate corruption scandals

Company	Estimated losses (US $)	Date	Scandal	Some impacts
Volkswagen	87 billion	2015	11 million cars worldwide fitted with a so-called defeat device that ran the car below normal power and performance when an emission test was occurring	Significant damage to Volkswagen's brand and the wider automotive sector
Petrobras	21 billion	2015	Alleged diversion of billions of dollars from company accounts for their executives use, or to pay off officials	Significant damage to Petrobras's brand and to Brazil's image as a destination for investment. Service providers have downgraded the companies' credit rating
Various international banks	9 billion (in fines)	2012	Manipulation of LIBOR interest rate benchmark	Fines and other prosecutions. Public loss of confidence may drive down the wider finance industry profits for years
Siemens	3 billion	2008	Payment of bribes for contracts	Significant loss of trust. Focus on improvements appears to have helped rebuild the company's reputation

Source: Adapted from Mooney et al. (2016, pp. 5–6)

Notwithstanding such a link with self-interest, I would consider this latter argument as a crucial one if one adheres, as I do, to the collaboration theory of the corporation expounded in chapter three. This theory views the corporation as a collaboration between the state and the individuals who organise, operate and own it to pursue the development of a common project, namely economic development and economic gain. By engaging in acts of corruption, the corporation is directly undermining both one of the members of the collective that is the corporation and the common project towards the realisation of which its members work.

I believe that Bommier and Renouard (2018) are on the right track when they link the fight against corruption to the preservation of the democratic ideal, which they view as an immaterial commons to be defended. These researchers refer to the responsibility corporations have concerning "the legitimacy of the democratic process, the sovereignty of states, and the social link" (p. 217). For them, both when they lobby for regulations that are beneficial to business but harmful to society and when they engage in actions of corruption, corporations are compromising democratic legitimacy and the social link. Regarding corruption, these researchers claim that "corruption scandals deeply affect the social link by reducing the trust citizens have in public administration and in their fellow citizens" (p. 231). Moreover, when such phenomenon extends to the private sector, "it is the trust in a market regulated with a view of the common good that slowly evaporates" (ibid).

Even disregarding these latter arguments and the fact that corruption is, at least for me, mainly an ethical problem, because corporations play a central role in the phenomenon of corruption, they could reap some benefits from the fight against corruption, such as those pertaining to reduction in costs, increase in operational efficiency and augmented reputation (Hills et al., 2009). Therefore, the fight against corruption offers a major opportunity to address an issue that is inherently linked with both corporate and societal interests via CSR policies and activities.

5.3.2 The Fight Against Corruption in CSR Instruments and Legislation

Nowadays, the fight against corruption is a full-fledged component of corporations' social responsibility policies and practices. Since corruption is detrimental to the pursuance of sustainable (human) development in view of the detrimental impacts it has, over the last few decades, one has witnessed the introduction and development of the fight against corruption in CSR instruments. I have already mentioned its consideration in the 2030 Agenda for Sustainable Development and SDGs. I will now address how the fight against corruption is considered in some CSR legislation, such as the 2014 European Union Non-Financial Reporting Directive (EU NFRD), and in relevant voluntary CSR initiatives, such as the OECD Guidelines for MNEs, the United Nations Global Compact (UNGC), ISO 26000 and the GRI Standards.

The European Union Approach to Anti-corruption

In the European Commission's Green Paper (European Commission, 2001), two dimensions of CSR were considered, an internal dimension and an external one. Each one of these dimensions was further divided into four components. Regarding the internal dimension, the following four components were considered: human resources management; health and safety at work; adaptation to change; management of environmental impacts and natural resources. As to the external dimension, it was divided into components pertaining to local communities; business partners, suppliers and consumers; human rights; and global environmental concerns. The topic of corruption was only mentioned in connection with the human rights component. In the 2002 communication (European Commission, 2002), which constituted a follow-up to the Green Paper, the fight against corruption was more explicitly addressed as a CSR issue. In this latter document, corporations were considered as being able to play a major role "in preventing and combating corruption and bribery, and in helping preventing the use of enterprises for money laundering and criminal activities financing" (p. 9).

But it was with the European Commission (2011) communication "A renewed EU strategy 2011–14 for Corporate Social Responsibility" that the fight against corruption became one of the main topics of CSR. In this document, the fight against corruption is explicitly acknowledged as one of the CSR main issues, along with human rights, labour and employment practices, and environmental issues.

This acknowledgement of the fight against corruption as one of the central issues of CSR became even more entrenched with the 2014 "Directive on the disclosure of non-financial information and information about diversity". This Directive makes mandatory to "large undertakings which are public-interest entities exceeding on their balance sheet dates the criterion of the average number of 500 employees during the financial year" to disclose information pertaining to "as a minimum, environmental, social and employee matters, respect for human rights, anti-corruption and bribery matters" (European Union, 2014).

In 2017, the European Commission published a document with the title "Guidelines on non-financial reporting (methodology for reporting non-financial information)" (European Commission, 2017). In this document, the European Commission emphasises that corporations are expected to "disclose material information on how they manage anti-corruption and bribery matters and occurrences" and suggests them to make disclosures on "organisation, decisions, management instruments, and on the resources allocated to fighting corruption and bribery" (p. 17). It furthermore asserts that corporations "may also consider explaining how they assess fighting corruption and bribery, take action to prevent or mitigate adverse impacts, monitor effectiveness, and communicate on the matter internally and externally" (ibid.). The European Commission also points to the usefulness of relying on "broadly recognized, high quality frameworks" such as the OECD Guidelines for MNEs or the ISO 26000.

One can also obtain from these guidelines on non-financial reporting reference to aspects regarding which corporations may consider disclosing material information and key performance indicators. They are the following (p. 17):

- anti-corruption policies, procedures and standards;
- criteria used in corruption-related risk assessments;
- internal control processes and resources allocated to preventing corruption and bribery;
- employees having received appropriate training;
- use of whistleblowing mechanisms;
- the number of pending or completed legal actions on anti-competitive behaviour.

The OECD Guidelines for Multinational Enterprises

The OECD Guidelines for MNEs, created in 1976 and revised a couple of times, the last revision dating from 2011, devote a chapter to "Combating Bribery, Bribe Solicitation and Extortion". In this chapter, on can find the following assertions regarding corporations' practices: they "should not directly or indirectly, offer, promise, give, or demand a bribe or other undue advantage to obtain or retain business or other improper advantage"; they "should also resist the solicitation of bribes and extortion". (OECD, 2011, p. 47). OECD then proceeds to state what corporations more specifically should do. According to the quick view OECD Watch (2013, p. 45) offers of the aforementioned chapter, corporations should:

- Not offer bribes, directly or indirectly, to obtain or retain business or other undue advantage, §1.
- Resist solicitation of bribes and extortion, §1.
- Not offer, promise or give undue monetary or other advantages to public officials or the employees of business partners directly or through intermediaries, e.g. agents, consultants, suppliers, §1.
- Adopt adequate internal controls based on risk assessment and financial and accounting procedures to prevent bribery, §2.
- Regularly monitor and re-assess bribery risks and the respective internal controls designed for the enterprise's specific circumstances and adapt the respective controls when necessary to ensure their continued effectiveness, §2.
- Prohibit or discourage the use of facilitation payments, and, when they are made, accurately record them in financial records so they cannot be used for bribing or hiding bribery, §3.
- Ensure properly documented due diligence when hiring and overseeing agents, ensuring that their remuneration is for legitimate services only, §4.
- Enhance the transparency and effectiveness of anti-bribery activities by making management commitments to combating bribery public and disclosing the internal control systems designed to achieve the pronounced aims, §5.
- Foster openness and dialogue with the public to promote its cooperation with the fight against bribery, §5.
- Promote employee awareness and compliance with anti-bribery policies and internal controls, §6.
- Refrain from making illegal contributions to candidates for public office, political parties or other political organisations, §7.

The OECD Guidelines for MNEs also include a chapter on "Disclosure", which encourages the disclosure of "timely and accurate information" pertaining to "all material matters regarding their activities, structure, financial situation, performance, ownership and governance" (OECD, 2011, p. 27).

When referring to the OECD Guidelines for MNEs, one also has to refer to the very recent OECD Due Diligence Guidance for Responsible Business Conduct (OECD, 2018). This is a document adopted in 2018 which aims at providing support to corporations on the implementation of the OECD Guidelines for MNEs. OECD (2018) addresses the issue of actual adverse impacts or potential adverse impacts (risks) pertaining to some of the topics covered in the OECD Guidelines for MNEs: human rights, employment and industrial relations, environment, combating bribery, bribe solicitation and extortion, consumer interests, and disclosure. OECD (2018, p. 21) recommends a six step approach to the due diligence process:

1. Embed responsible business conduct into policies and management systems.
2. Identify and assess adverse impacts in operations, supply chains, and business relationships.
3. Cease, prevent, or mitigate adverse impacts.
4. Track implementation and results.
5. Communicate how impacts are addressed.
6. Provide for or cooperate in remediation when appropriate.

Regarding the topic of bribery, bribe solicitation and extortion, one of the relevant pieces of information in this OECD document pertains to examples of adverse

Table 5.4 Examples of indicators of scale, scope and irremediable character regarding corruption

Examples of scale	Examples of scope	Examples of the irremediable character
– Monetary amount of the bribe – Loss of life or severe bodily harm caused by bribery – Criminal nature of the bribe – Extent of impact on markets, people, environment and society due to decisions made based on bribery – Size of the profit gained from the bribery	– Frequency at which bribes are paid – Geographic spread of bribery – Number and/or level of officials, employees or agents engaged in bribery – Extent of activities linked with bribery – Number of identifiable groups impacted by decisions based on bribery	– Extent of damage to society due to loss of public funds – Extent to which activities undertaken and enabled by bribery will lead to irremediable adverse impacts

Source: Adapted from OECD (2018, p. 43)

impacts. OECD (2018, p. 40) includes the following list of such examples: bribery of public officials to win public procurement contracts; bribery of public officials to obtain favourable tax treatment or other preferential treatment or access to confidential information; bribery of public officials to obtain customs clearance; bribery of public officials to obtain authorisations or permits; selling products to government agencies at an elevated price to provide public officials with a share of the profit; bribing public officials to ignore or avoid regulations or controls; providing gifts, meals and entertainment to those with whom the enterprise does business without adequate controls or records; receiving gifts from business partners or public officials without adequate controls or record.

According to the guidance offered by OECD (2018, p. 42), given that responsibility for addressing the adverse impacts which they have caused or contributed to, when the corporation cannot address simultaneously all such impacts it has identified, it should "prioritise the order in which it takes action based on the severity and likelihood" of the impact. The severity of the adverse impacts will be assessed in terms of scale (gravity of the impact), scope (reach of the adverse impact) and irremediable character ("limits on the ability to restore the individuals or environment affected to a situation equivalent to their situation before the adverse impact") (ibid.). In OECD (2018), a set of examples of indicators of scale, scope and irremediable character is offered (Table 5.4).

Another relevant aspect which is addressed in OECD (2018, p. 50) pertains to the fact that in the case of corruption (as is the case also with greenhouse gas emissions), adverse impacts "result in collective harms". In such a case, it may prove impossible to individually engage with individually potentially impacted stakeholders. In these circumstances, it may be useful to engage with "credible stakeholder representatives or proxy organisations (e.g. NGOs, representative public bodies, etc.)" (p. 51).

The United Nations Global Compact

The original nine principles of the UNGC cover topics in human rights, labour and environment (UNGC, 2008). A tenth principle relating to anti-corruption was added

Fig. 5.2 UNGC's management model. Source: Brew et al. (2011, p. 9)

in 2004, providing that "businesses should work against corruption in all its forms, including extortion and bribery" (ibid.).

The UNGC suggests to participants to consider the following the UNGC Management Model in their fight against corruption and implementation of the tenth principle (Brew et al., 2011). Such a model consists of six steps and is presented in Fig. 5.2.

As argued by Côté-Freeman and Fagan (2010), the credibility of CSR initiatives that address corruption requires companies to communicate and be more transparent about their efforts pertaining to the fight against corruption with internal and external stakeholders.

In 2009, the UNGC, in partnership with TI, published a document with the title "Reporting Guidance on the 10th Principle Against Corruption" (UNGC/TI, 2009). This document is much more detailed than the GRI Standard on anti-corruption, which will be addressed below. It provides a set of 22 "reporting elements", which

Table 5.5 UNGC tenth principle guidance

Category	Reporting elements (B: basic; D: desired)
Commitment and policy	B1 Publicly stated commitment to work against corruption in all its forms, including bribery and extortion B2 Commitment to be in compliance with all relevant laws, including anti-corruption laws D1 Publicly stated formal policy of zero-tolerance of corruption D2 Statement of support for international and regional legal frameworks, such as the UN Convention against Corruption D3 Carrying out risk assessment of potential areas of corruption D4 Detailed policies for high-risk areas of corruption D5 Policy on anti-corruption regarding business partners
Implementation	B3 Translation of the anti-corruption commitment into actions B4 Support by the organisation's leadership for anti-corruption B5 Communication and training on the anti-corruption commitment for all employees B6 Internal checks and balances to ensure consistency with the anti-corruption commitment D6 Actions taken to encourage business partners to implement anti-corruption commitments D7 Management responsibility and accountability for implementation of the anti-corruption commitment or policy D8 Human Resources procedures supporting the anti-corruption commitment or policy D9 Communications (whistleblowing) channels and follow-up mechanisms for reporting concerns or seeking advice D10 Internal accounting and auditing procedures related to anti-corruption D11 Participation in voluntary anti-corruption initiatives
Monitoring	B7 Monitoring and improvement processes D12 Leadership review of monitoring and improvement results D13 Dealing with incidents D14 Public legal cases regarding corruption D15 Use of independent external assurance of anti-corruption programs

Source: Adapted from UNGC/TI (2009, p. 14)

are classified as "basic" or "desired" and cover the following categories: "commitment and policy"; "implementation"; and "monitoring". They are presented in Table 5.5.

ISO 26000

The ISO 26000 (ISO, 2010) provides guidance concerning the issues "anti-corruption" and "responsible political engagement" in the core subject "fair operating practices". The issues listed under this core subject include, besides the two mentioned above (issues 1 and 2, respectively), "fair competition" (issue 3); "promoting social responsibility in the value chain" (issue 4), and "respect for property rights" (issue 5).

Fair operating practices are described as concerning "ethical conduct in an organization's dealings with other organizations". Such dealings "include relationships between organizations and government agencies, as well as between organizations and their partners, suppliers, contractors, customers, competitors, and the associations of which they are members".

ISO 26000 defines corruption as "the abuse of entrusted power for private gain. Corruption can take many forms. Examples of corruption include bribery (soliciting, offering or accepting a bribe in money or in kind) involving public officials or people in the private sector, conflict of interest, fraud, money laundering, embezzlement, concealment and obstruction of justice, and trading in influence".

Regarding responsible political involvement, this standard asserts that "organizations can support public political processes and encourage the development of public policy that benefits society at large". Notwithstanding, they "should prohibit use of undue influence and avoid behaviour, such as manipulation, intimidation and coercion, that can undermine the public political process".

Regarding both these issues, ISO 26000 provides a set of "related actions and expectations" that include, in both cases, the training of employees regarding them. Regarding anti-corruption, the identification of risks is one of the actions and expectations identified. In the case of political involvement, ISO 26000 refers, among other actions and expectations, to the importance of transparency pertaining to such involvement. I should also mention that ISO has produced a document establishing the linkages between ISO 26000 and the OECD Guidelines for MNEs (ISO, 2017).

GRI Standards

Regarding the GRI Standards/Guidelines, I will refer to the topics of corruption/anti-corruption and political contributions/public policy for reasons presented above. One of such reasons is that the OECD Guidelines for MNEs consider this latter aspect in the chapter pertaining to corruption (Chapter VII—Combating Bribery, Bribe Solicitation and Extortion). Hence, when trying to establish a link between the OECD Guidelines for MNEs and the GRI Standards/Guidelines, one has to consider not only the GRI's disclosure items and/or indicators on anti-corruption, but also the one on public policy (Table 5.6). This has been precisely what has been done in the

Table 5.6 Linking the UNGC tenth principle, the OECD Guidelines for MNEs, the UE NFRD, and the GRI Standards

UNGC (10th principle)	OECD Guidelines (Chapter VII)	ISO 26000	UE NFRD	GRI Standards
Businesses should work against corruption in all its forms, including extortion and bribery	Enterprises should not, directly or indirectly, offer, promise, give, or demand a bribe or other undue advantage to obtain or retain business or other improper advantage. Nor should enterprises be solicited or expected to render a bribe or other undue advantage	Fair operating practices 1. Anti-corruption 2. Responsible political involvement	Anti-corruption and bribery	GRI 205: Anti-corruption GRI 415: Public Policy

only document that I am aware of that establishes a link between the OECD Guidelines for MNEs and the GRI Guidelines (GRI, 2004).

In the first version of the GRI Guidelines (GRI, 2000), the issue of corruption was not treated. In the second version (G2) (GRI, 2002), only three indicators related to the fight against corruption were proposed. One related to "bribery and corruption": SO2—description of the policy, procedures/management systems, and compliance mechanisms for organisations and employees addressing bribery and corruption. The other two pertaining to "political contributions": SO3—description of policy, procedures/management systems, and compliance mechanisms for managing political lobbying and contributions; SO5—amount of money paid to political parties and institutions whose prime function is to fund political parties or their candidates.

In the third version of the guidelines (G3 and G3.1), "bribery and corruption" and "political contributions" were renamed "corruption" and "public policy". The importance of anti-corruption has increased, and five indicators were proposed (GRI, 2006, 2011) (Table 5.7). In the fourth version of the GRI Guidelines (G4) (GRI, 2013), the "corruption" aspect was renamed "anti-corruption", and four of the indicators proposed in the G3.1 version have been substantially developed (Table 5.7).

Some changes in the approach occurred with the GRI Standards (GRI, 2020). One of the changes was that the anti-corruption issue is now considered within the economic aspect rather than within the social one. GRI 205: Anti-corruption is an economic standard. The public policy issue is still considered a social aspect, and GRI 415: Public Policy is a social standard. In Table 5.8, the disclosures and reporting requirements proposed by these two standards are presented in some detail.

It is important to note that the topic of public policy includes, as mentioned in GRI's 415 background context, "participation in the development of public policy through activities such as lobbying and making financial or in-kind contributions to political parties, politicians, or causes" (GRI, 2020). Regarding management approach disclosures, GRI's 415 reporting recommendations specify that the organisation should report "the significant issues that are the focus of its participation in public policy development and lobbying", as well as "its stance on these issues, and any differences between its lobbying positions and any stated policies, goals, or other public positions" (ibid.).

GRI has made an initial effort to provide guidance on integrating the OECD Guidelines with the GRI Guidelines, offering a guide to help organisations communicate their use of the OECD Guidelines using the 2002 version of the GRI guidelines (GRI, 2004). It seems to have been a one-time-only effort instead of an on-going project. Although four versions of the GRI guidelines have been produced, and in 2016 the GRI Standards were created, the 2004 document has not been updated until now.

On the contrary, albeit it has not been revised to take into account the GRI Standards, the connection between the GRI Guidelines and the UNGC has been the object of an on-going effort. The first document providing a link between the UNGC and the GRI Guidelines was the 2007 document "Making the connection—The GRI Guidelines and the Global Compact Communication on Progress" (UNGC/

Table 5.7 Anti-corruption and public policy indicators in GRI G3.1 and G4 Guidelines

	Indicators	
Aspects	G3.1	G4
Corruption/Anti-corruption	SO2—Percentage and total number of business units analysed for risks related to corruption	**SO3 – Total number and percentage of operations assessed for risks related to corruption and the significant risks identified** a. Report the total number and percentage of operations assessed for risks related to corruption b. Report the significant risks related to corruption identified through the risk assessment
	SO3—Percentage of employees trained in organisation's anti-corruption policies and procedures	**SO4 – Communication and training on anti-corruption policies and procedures** a. Report the total number and percentage of governance body members that the organisation's anti-corruption policies and procedures have been communicated to, broken down by region b. Report the total number and percentage of employees that the organisation's anti-corruption policies and procedures have been communicated to, broken down by employee category and region c. Report the total number and percentage of business partners that the organisation's anti-corruption policies and procedures have been communicated to, broken down by type of business partner and region d. Report the total number and percentage of governance body members that have received training on anti-corruption, broken down by region e. Report the total number and percentage of employees that have received training on anti-corruption, broken down by employee category and region
	SO4—Actions taken in response to incidents of corruption	**SO5—Confirmed incidents of corruption and actions taken** a. Report the total number and nature of confirmed incidents of corruption b. Report the total number of confirmed incidents in which employees were dismissed or disciplined for corruption c. Report the total number of confirmed incidents when contracts with business partners were terminated or not renewed due to violations related to corruption d. Report public legal cases regarding corruption brought against the organisation or its employees during the reporting period and the outcomes of such cases
Public Policy	SO5—Public policy positions and participation in public policy development and lobbying	**SO6 – Total value of political contributions by country and recipient/beneficiary** a. Report the total monetary value of financial and in-kind political contributions made directly and indirectly by the organisation by country and recipient/beneficiary b. Report how the monetary value of in-kind contributions was estimated, if applicable
	SO6—Total value of financial and in-kind contributions to political parties, politicians, and related institutions by country	

Table 5.8 Anti-corruption and public policy in GRI Standards

Standards	Disclosures	Reporting requirements
GRI 205: Anti-corruption	Management approach disclosures	Management approach for anti-corruption using GRI 103: Management Approach
	Disclosure 205-1 Operations assessed for risks related to corruption	a. Total number and percentage of operations assessed for risks related to corruption b. Significant risks related to corruption identified through the risk assessment
	Disclosure 205-2 Communication and training about anti-corruption policies and procedures	a. Total number and percentage of governance body members that the organisation's anti-corruption policies and procedures have been communicated to, broken down by region b. Total number and percentage of employees that the organisation's anti-corruption policies and procedures have been communicated to, broken down by employee category and region c. Total number and percentage of business partners that the organisation's anti-corruption policies and procedures have been communicated to, broken down by type of business partner and region. Describe if the organisation's anti-corruption policies and procedures have been communicated to any other persons or organisations d. Total number and percentage of governance body members that have received training on anti-corruption, broken down by region e. Total number and percentage of employees that have received training on anti-corruption, broken down by employee category and region
	Disclosure 205-3 Confirmed incidents of corruption and actions taken	a. Total number and nature of confirmed incidents of corruption b. Total number of confirmed incidents in which employees were dismissed or disciplined for corruption c. Total number of confirmed incidents when contracts with business partners were terminated or not renewed due to violations related to corruption d. Public legal cases regarding corruption brought against the organisation or its employees during the reporting period and the outcomes of such cases
GRI 415: Public Policy	Management approach disclosures	Management approach for public policy using GRI 103: Management Approach
	Disclosure 415-1 Political contributions	a. Total monetary value of financial and in-kind political contributions made directly and indirectly by the organisation by country and recipient/beneficiary b. If applicable, how the monetary value of in-kind contributions was estimated

GRI, 2007), in which an important effort to provide guidance on integrating the COP with sustainability reports elaborated in accordance with G3 version of the GRI Guidelines was provided (UNGC/GRI, 2007). The most recent document that I am aware of regarding this matter was published in 2014 with the title "Making the Connection: Using the GRI G4 Guidelines to Communicate Progress on the UN Global Compact Principles" (UNGC/GRI, 2013).

I should also mention the efforts to establish the link between the GRI Standards/ Guidelines and the UE NFRD. GRI (2015) aims at showing how GRI G4 Guidelines can be used by corporations to comply with the EU NFRD, whereas GRI (2017) purports to pursue the same aim regarding the GRI Standards.

Other Relevant Instruments

I would not like to end this section without mentioning briefly a well-established anti-corruption instrument, the Extractive Industries Transparency Initiative (EITI), and two very recent instruments, the WEF "Measuring Stakeholder Capitalism—Towards Common Metrics and Consistent Reporting of Sustainable Value Creation" (in collaboration with Deloitte, EY, KPMG and PwC) and the Transparency International UK's (2020) "Principles and guidance for anti-corruption corporate transparency".

The EITI is a voluntary multi-stakeholder initiative involving governments, civil society organisations and corporations in the extractive industries, first launched in 2003 (Aaronson, 2011; Kleizen, 2019; Sovacool et al., 2016). In terms of the attention paid by governments, corporations and civil society organisations to transparency as a way of fighting corruption and tax evasion and avoidance, this is one of the better known and more influential initiatives. Aaronson (2011, p. 52) refers to the EITI as a public–private partnership aimed at curbing corruption and improving government. This initiative requires, inter alia, disclosure by governments of the income received from corporations in the oil, gas and mining sectors and expects disclosure by supporting corporations of payments to the governments of the countries in which they operate.

I have already referred to Transparency International UK's (2020) approach to anti-corruption reporting (in the introductory chapter to this book). It has been an approach of identifying five key areas considered of high risk of corporate corruption and providing guidance on disclosure pertaining to them. These areas are as follows:

- Anti-corruption programmes.
- Beneficial ownership.
- Organisational structure.
- Country-by-country reporting.
- Corporate political engagement.

Transparency International UK (2020) provides a set of very detailed principles for reporting on anti-corruption programmes that address the following topics: top-level commitment to anti-bribery and corruption; anti-bribery and corruption policies; risk assessment; human resources; conflict of interest; charitable donations and sponsorships; facilitation payments; gifts and hospitality; training; monitoring and review; whistleblowing; dealing with incidents; managing third parties; and private procurement transparency. Regarding the principles for political engagement transparency, besides offering some guidance regarding the control environment, Transparency International UK focuses on lobbying, political contributions, and the revolving door phenomenon.

WEF (2020) includes the aspects of anti-corruption and lobbying under the theme "Ethical behaviour". It distinguishes between "core metrics and disclosures" and "expanded metrics and disclosures". The first pertains to "more-established or critically important metrics and disclosures", which are primarily quantitative in nature and concern types of information that are already being reported by numerous corporations or are likely to be procured without great effort and focus (p. 6). The second concerns less well-established types of information that "have a wider value chain scope or convey impact in a more sophisticated or tangible way, such as in monetary terms." (ibid.) These latter metrics and disclosures "represent a more advanced way of measuring and communicating sustainable value creation". (ibid.)

Regarding anti-corruption, the WEF (2020, p. 51) proposes the following "core metrics and disclosures":

1. Total percentage of governance body members, employees and business partners who have received training on the organization's anti-corruption policies and procedures, broken down by region.
2. (a) Total number and nature of incidents of corruption confirmed during the current year, but related to previous years; and
   (b) Total number and nature of incidents of corruption confirmed during the current year, related to this year.
3. Discussion of initiatives and stakeholder engagement to improve the broader operating environment and culture, in order to combat corruption.

Regarding lobbying, WEF (2020, p. 54) proposes the following "expanded metrics and disclosures": "The significant issues that are the focus of the company's participation in public policy development and lobbying; the company's strategy relevant to these areas of focus; and any differences between its lobbying positions and its purpose, stated policies, goals or other public positions". As one can see, the metrics and disclosures pertaining to the issues examined here proposed by WEF (2020) are strongly influenced by the GRI Standards. It is, however, interesting to note that there is no reference whatsoever to political contributions in WEF (2020).

5.3.3 Some Evidence Regarding Anti-corruption Reporting

According to the UNGC/TI (2009, p. 2), "transparency is a first-line defence against corruption", and public reporting may be considered as being "a formalization of transparency". Anti-corruption reporting is viewed by many as crucial in the fight against corruption (Klitgaard, 1998; Halter et al., 2009; Hess, 2012). Transparency International (TI, 2009, p. 4) suggests that the degree of such reporting "can, in most cases, be a strong indicator of the quality and comprehensiveness of a company's efforts in addressing bribery corruption".

Referring to CSR reporting in general, Graafland and Smid (2019) argue that higher-quality reporting helps to strengthen the quality of corporations' CSR programs. According to these researchers, "by fostering transparency, reporting will stimulate companies to narrow the gap between policies and impacts" (p. 261). Regarding the specific case of anti-corruption reporting, Hess (2009) puts forward a similar perspective. This author suggests that such type of reporting may constitute an important tool in helping corporations to understand what works in anti-corruption efforts and achieve more developed risk assessments, and also as a way to ensure that corporations' leaders are held accountable to the public with respect to performance on that field and to pressure other similar companies to adopt anti-corruption principles.

About 15 years ago, Wilkinson (2006, p. 102) emphasised that one could not consider the reporting on the efforts regarding the fight against corruption as having such a long history as environmental reporting. Not only corruption is by its very nature "secret, hidden and viewed as sensitive by companies", but also its scope is wide (the areas it encompasses range from bribery to money laundering) (ibid.). In addition, "from the perspective of the general public, the topic is complex and does not carry the same emotive weight as human rights" (ibid.).

In the last decade, a number of studies surveying the state of anti-corruption reporting around the world have been published by important organisations devoted to the fight against corruption, such as Transparency International, and to NFR, such as the Alliance for Corporate Transparency. In what follows, I will present the mains results of some of these studies.

In chapter four, I mentioned a recent study examining the implementation of the EU NFRD (Alliance for Corporate Transparency, 2020), which presents evidence on the NFR practices of 1000 European companies. Overall, the findings of this study suggest that although such reporting is widespread (with 19 out of 20 companies reporting such information), there is a problem concerning companies reporting policies rather than results, which leads to the claim that there is a "failure to address concrete issues, targets and principal risks" (p. 4).

Alliance for Corporate Transparency (2020, pp. 90–91) provides evidence on anti-corruption reporting regarding policies, outcomes, and risks. Whilst 88.1% of the corporations describe their anti-corruption policies, only 19.7% report on key issues and objectives. The analysis of the specific topics addressed in such policies revealed that in spite of 76.1% of the corporations expresses commitment to anti-corruption, only a minority are specific concerning who the policies apply to (Table 5.9). Noteworthily, the percentage of corporations describing the main elements of their programmes on the fight against corruption is only 33.7.

Regarding policy outcomes, only 46% provide some description (which contrasts with the 88.1% reporting on policies), and only 5.9% describe the outcomes in terms of meeting policy targets (the other 40.1% being vague about it). Worthy of mention is the fact that only 6.7% of the corporations provide evidence of effective management of incidents and cases (Table 5.9).

Table 5.9 Specific aspects addressed in anti-corruption policies

Aspects	%
Policies' specific aspects	
Commitment to anti-corruption and bribery	76.1
A-C policy explicitly apply to persons authorised to act on behalf of the company	25.0
A-C policy apply to non-controlled persons or entities under contract	39.5
A-C policy includes rules on gifts and hospitality/expenses	46.4
A-C policy explicitly prohibits facilitation of payments	28.4
Main elements of the dedicated anti-corruption programme (A-C)	33.7
Outcomes description	
Number of incidents	35.1
Description of concrete cases	4.9
Evidence of effective management	6.7
Identified risks	
Monitoring of A-C programme's effectiveness	15.0
Data on employees' trust in effectiveness of the company's anti-corruption	1.7
Risks assessment of potential areas of corruption	18.3
Internal check and balances to ensure consistency with the A-C commitment	16.2
Actions to encourage business partners to implement A-C commitment	22.6
Info on all current public investigations, prosecutions or closed	7.2

Source: Based on Alliance for Corporate Transparency (2020, pp. 90–91)

Concerning identified risks, 35.1% of the corporations do not provide information on them, and of those that provide such information, only 20.5% describe specific risks. Another finding worthy of note is that only 18.3% of the corporations disclose information on how the risks of potential areas of corruption are assessed (Table 5.9).

At least since 2009, TI has been preparing studies on transparency in corporate reporting (TRAC), including anti-corruption reporting. This organisation has built a methodology for corporate transparency based on the experience of two of its previous projects: "Transparency in Reporting on Anti-Corruption" and "Promoting Revenue Transparency". Three TI publications have their origins in these projects: TI (2009) in the first project; TI (2008) and TI (2011) in the latter project. The methodology for the assessment of corporate transparency has been used in the more recent studies of the project, TI (2012), TI (2013), TI (2014), and TI (2016). In these latter studies, in addition to assessments on country-by-country reporting and organisational transparency, evidence of the level of anti-corruption reporting is provided. TI (2012, 2014) focus on the largest publicly traded multinational corporations (based on market value), and TI (2013, 2016) assess transparency in corporate reporting of emerging market multinationals. Meanwhile, several studies focusing on multinationals from given countries have been produced by TI national chapters using this same methodology. Over 20 of these reports have been published (Weber, 2019).

Table 5.10 TRAC tool questions regarding anti-corruption reporting

1. Does the company have a publicly stated commitment to anti-corruption?
2. Does the company publicly commit to be in compliance with all relevant laws, including anti-corruption laws?
3. Does the company leadership (senior member of management or board) demonstrate support for anti-corruption?
4. Does the company's code of conduct/anti-corruption policy explicitly apply to all employees and directors?
5. Does the company's anti-corruption policy explicitly apply to persons who are not employees but are authorised to act on behalf of the company or represent it (for example: agents, advisors, representatives or intermediaries)?
6. Does the company's anti-corruption programme apply to non-controlled persons or entities that provide goods or services under contract (for example: contractors, subcontractors, suppliers)?
7. Does the company have in place an anti-corruption training programme for its employees and directors?
8. Does the company have a policy on gifts, hospitality and expenses?
9. Is there a policy that explicitly prohibits facilitation payments?
10. Does the programme enable employees and others to raise concerns and report violations (of the programme) without risk of reprisal?
11. Does the company provide a channel through which employees can report suspected breaches of anti-corruption policies, and does the channel allow for confidential and/or anonymous reporting (whistleblowing)?
12. Does the company carry out regular monitoring of its anti-corruption programme to review the programme's suitability, adequacy and effectiveness, and implement improvements as appropriate?
13. Does the company have a policy on political contributions that either prohibits such contributions or, if it does not, requires such contributions to be publicly disclosed?

Regarding reporting on anti-corruption programs, the TRAC tool assesses such reporting based on thirteen questions derived from UNGC/TI (2009), presented above (Table 5.10). According to Weber (2019, p. 16), this tool "is valued as one of the most important and visible advocacy tools developed by Transparency International".

In Table 5.11, a summary of the average anti-corruption reporting score as reported in the TI reports, both those prepared by TI regarding global multinational corporations and those prepared by TI national chapters, is provided. Table 5.11 is based on Weber (2019, p. 77). Regarding the information presented by this researcher, I only include in the table under consideration information based on the most recent TI national chapter TRAC report in the cases in which two or more reports have been published (Belgium, Denmark, Lithuania, the Netherlands, and South Africa). Given that some reports have been published subsequently to the publication of Weber's study, I have included the new information based on these new reports. It is interesting to note that the countries evidencing a higher average rate of reporting are countries appearing in the CPI as ranking low in terms of perceptions of corruption, such as Denmark, the Netherlands, Sweden, and the UK

Table 5.11 Anti-corruption reporting (ACR) in TRAC reports

Year	No. Assessed corporations	Average results ACR (%)
Panel A—Global		
2009	500	47
2012	105	68
2014	124	70
Panel B—EMM		
2013	100	46
2016	100	48
Country/Year	No. assessed corporations	Average results ACR (%)
Panel C—Local		
Belgium (2016)	27	27
Brazil (2018)	110	65
Chile (2014)	19	48
Denmark (2016)	30	75
Greece (2016)	16	39
Italy (2013)	15	67
Hungary (2013)	50	45
Kuwait (2013)	4	40
Lithuania (2017)	49	32
Netherlands (2019)[a]	29	68
Norway (2013)	50	54
Russia (2018)	200	27
South Africa (2020)[a]	100	59
South Korea (2016)	50	56
Sweden (2013)	20	75
Si Lanka (2020)[a]	50	27
Turkey (2015)	100	28
UK (2015)	33	67
Ukraine (2016)	100	20
Vietnam (2018)	45	15

[a]Information directly obtained in the TRAC report
Source: Adapted from Weber (2019, p. 77)

(75%, 68%, 68%, and 67%, respectively). It is, however, also worthy of note the relatively high levels of reporting in countries with which one associate high levels of corruption, such as Brazil and South Africa (65% and 59%, respectively). Notwithstanding, one must not forget that these two latter countries have two of the largest capital markets in the world and are the home of some of the largest multinational corporations.

References

Aaronson, S. A. (2011). Limited partnership: Business, government, civil society, and the public in the extractive industries transparency initiative (EITI). *Public Administration and Development, 31*(1), 50–63.

Aguilera, R., & Abhijeet, V. (2008). The dark side of authority: Antecedents, mechanisms, and outcomes of organizational corruption. *Journal of Business Ethics, 77*(4), 431–449.

Aidt, T. S. (2011). Corruption and sustainable development. In S. Rose-Ackerman & T. Søreide (Eds.), *International handbook on the economics of corruption* (Vol. 2, pp. 3–51). Edward Elgar.

Aidt, T. S. (2016). Rent seeking and the economics of corruption. *Constitutional Political Economy, 27*(2), 142–157.

Alliance for Corporate Transparency. (2020). Research Report 2019: An analysis of the sustainability reports of 1000 companies pursuant to the EU Non-Financial Reporting Directive. Alliance for Corporate Transparency.

Argandoña, A. (2003). Private-to-private corruption. *Journal of Business Ethics, 47*(3), 253–267.

Argandoña, A. (2005). Corruption and companies: The use of facilitating payments. *Journal of Business Ethics, 603*, 251–264.

Argandoña, A. (2007). The United Nations Convention Against Corruption and its Impact on International Companies. *Journal of Business Ethics, 74*, 481–496.

Bommier, S., & Renouard, C. (2018). *L'Entreprise Comme Commun: Au-Delà de la RSE*. Éditions Charles Léopold Mayer.

Brew, P., Chung, D. W., Cote-Freeman, S., Horowitz, B., Makinwa, O., Trott, A., & Wilkinson, P. (2011). *Business against corruption – A framework for action*. United Nations Global Compact/International Business Leaders Forum/Transparency International.

Castro, A., Phillips, N., & Ansari, S. (2020). Corporate corruption: A review and an agenda for future research. *Academy of Management Annals, 14*(2), 935–968.

Choudhury, B., & Petrin, M. (2019). *Corporate duties to the public*. Cambridge University Press.

Christensen, J. (2011). The looting continues: Tax havens and corruption. *Critical Perspectives on International Business., 7*(2), 177–196.

Côté-Freeman, S., & Fagan, C. (2010). *Corporate responsibility & anti-corruption: The missing link?* Transparency International Working Paper # 01/2010.

Dion, M. (2010). Corruption and ethical relativism: What is at stake? *Journal of Financial Crime, 172*, 240–250.

Errath, B., Brew, P., Moberg, J., & Brooks, J. (2005). *Business against corruption – A framework for action*. United Nations Global Compact/Prince of Wales International Business Leaders Forum/Transparency International.

European Commission. (2001). *Green paper – Promoting a European framework for corporate social responsibility*. COM(2001). 366 final.

European Commission. (2002). *Corporate social responsibility: A business contribution to sustainable development*. COM(2002). 347 final.

European Commission. (2011). Communication from the Commission to the European Parliament, the Council, the European Economic and Social Committee and the Committee of the Regions. A renewed EU strategy 2011–14 for Corporate Social Responsibility. COM 2011(681) final.

European Commission. (2017). *Communication from the Commission—Guidelines on non-financial reporting (methodology for reporting non-financial information)*. 2017/C 215/01. Official Journal of the European Union.

European Union. (2014). Directive 2014/95/EU of the European Parliament and of the Council of 22 October 2014 amending Directive 2013/34/EU as regards disclosure of non-financial and diversity information by certain large undertakings and groups. Official Journal of the European Union.

Fjeldstad, O.-H., Jacobsen, S. K., Ringstad, P. H., & Ngowi, H.P. (Eds). (2017). Lifting the veil of secrecy: Perspectives on International Taxation and Capital Flight from Africa. Chr. Michelsen Institute.

Fleming, P., & Zyglidopoulos, S. C. (2009). *Charting corporate corruption: Agency, structure and escalation*. Cheltenham: Edward Elgar Publishing.

Fisman, R., & Miguel, E. (2008). *Economic Gangsters: Corruption, Violence, and the Poverty of Nations*. Princeton University Press.

Gopinath, C. (2008). Recognizing and justifying private corruption. *Journal of Business Ethics, 82*, 747–754.

Graafland, J., & Smid, H. (2019). Decoupling among CSR policies, programs, and impacts: An empirical study. *Business & Society, 58*(2), 231–267.

Graycar, A. (2015). Corruption: Classification and analysis. *Policy and Society, 34*(2), 87–96.

Graycar, A., & Monaghan, O. (2015). Rich country corruption. *International Journal of Public Administration, 38*(8), 586–595.

GRI. (2000). *Sustainability reporting guidelines*. GRI.

GRI. (2002). *Sustainability reporting guidelines*. GRI.

GRI. (2004). *Synergies between the OECD guidelines for multinational enterprises and the GRI sustainability reporting guidelines*. GRI.

GRI. (2006). *Sustainability reporting guidelines*. GRI.

GRI. (2011). *Sustainability reporting guidelines – G3.1*. GRI.

GRI (2013). *Sustainability reporting guidelines – G4*. GRI.

GRI. (2015). *Making Headway in Europe*. Linking GRI's G4 Guidelines and the European Directive on Non-financial and Diversity Disclosure. GRI

GRI. (2017). *Linking the GRI Standards and the European Directive on non-financial and diversity disclosure*. GRI.

GRI. (2020). *Consolidated set of GRI sustainability reporting standards 2020*. GRI.

Habib, M., & Zurawicki, L. (2001). Country-level investments and the effect of corruption – Some empirical evidence. *International Business Review, 10*, 687–700.

Halter, M. V., Arruda, M. C. C., & Halter, R. B. (2009). Transparency to reduce corruption? *Journal of Business Ethics, 84*, 373–385.

Hess, D. (2009). Catalyzing corporate commitment to combating corruption. *Journal of Business Ethics, 88*(4), 781–790.

Hess, D. (2012). Combating corruption through corporate transparency: Using enforcement discretion to improve disclosure. *Minnesota Journal of International Law, 21*, 42–70.

Hills, G., Fiske, L., & Mahmud, A. (2009). *Anti-corruption as strategic CSR: A call to action for corporations*. FSG Social Impact Advisors.

Hodgson, G. M. (2013). *From pleasure machines to moral communities: An evolutionary economics without homo economicus*. University of Chicago Press.

International Monetary Fund (IMF). (2019). *Fiscal monitor: Curbing corruption*. IMF.

International Organization for Standardization (ISO). (2010). *ISO 26000*. ISO.

International Organization for Standardization (ISO). (2017). *ISO 26000 and OECD guidelines*. Practical overview of the linkages. ISO.

Kleizen, B. (2019). Victims of their own success abroad? Why the withdrawal of US transparency rules is hindered by diffusion to the EU and Canada. *Journal of European Public Policy, 26*(3), 446–467.

Klitgaard, R. (1998). International cooperation against corruption. *Finance, Development, 35*(1), 3–6.

Linder, C., & Linder, R. (2008). Does business corruption have to be considered in all cases as moral misconduct? *Journal of Business Systems, Governance and Ethics, 3*(2), 1–16.

López Claros, A. (2015). Removing impediments to sustainable economic development: The case of corruption. *Journal of International Commerce, Economics and Policy, 6*(01), 1550002.

López Claros, A. (2017). The moral dimension of the fight against corruption. *Georgetown Journal of International Affairs, 18*(2), 33–40.

Menocal, R. A., Taxell, N., Johnsøn, J. S., Schmaljohann, M., Montero, A. G., De Simone, F., & Tobias, J. (2015). *Why corruption matters: Understanding causes, effects and how to address them*. Evidence Paper on Corruption. UK Department for International Development.

Mooney, O., Navarro Perez, M., Makinwa, O., & Goldsmith, M. (2016). *Engaging on anti-bribery and corruption: A guide for investors and companies*. PRI & UNGC.

Mugellini, G., & Villeneuve, J. P. (2019). Monitoring the risk of corruption at international level: The case of the United Nations sustainable development goals. *European Journal of Risk Regulation, 10*(1), 201–207.

O'Hara, P. A. (2014). Political economy of systemic and micro-corruption throughout the world. *Journal of Economic Issues, 48*(2), 279–308.

OECD. (2011). *The OECD guidelines for multinational enterprises*, 2011 Edition. OECD.

OECD. (2014). *OECD foreign bribery report*. An Analysis of the Crime of Bribery of Foreign Public Officials. OECD.

OECD. (2018). *OECD due diligence guidance for responsible business conduct*. OECD.

OECD Watch. (2013). *Calling for corporate accountability: A guide to the 2011 OECD guidelines for multinational enterprises*. OECD Watch.

Palan, R., Murphy, R., & Chavagneux, C. (2010). *Tax havens: How globalisation really works*. Ithaca, NY: Cornell University Press.

Pope, J. (2000). *Confronting corruption: The elements of a national integrity system (Transparency International Source Book)*. Transparency International.

Rabl, T., & Kühlmann, T. M. (2009). Why or why not? Rationalizing corruption in organizations. *Cross Cultural Management: An International Journal, 16*(3), 268–286.

Rodriguez, P., Siegel, D. S., Hillman, A., & Eden, L. (2006). Three lenses on the multinational enterprise: Politics, corruption and corporate social responsibility. *Journal of International Business Studies, 37*(6), 733–746.

Rose-Ackerman, S. (2002). "Grand" corruption and the ethics of global business. *Journal of Banking and Finance, 26*, 1889–1918.

Sampson, S. (2019). Anti-corruption: Who cares? In S. Arvidsson (Ed.), *Challenges in managing sustainable business* (pp. 277–294). Palgrave Mcmillan.

Sovacool, B. K., Walter, G., de Graaf, V., & T. e Andrews, N. (2016). Energy governance, transnational rules, and the resource curse: Exploring the effectiveness of the extractive industries transparency initiative (EITI). *World Development, 83*, 179–192.

Tanzi, V. (1998). Corruption around the world – Causes, consequences, scope, and cures. *IMF Staff Papers, 454*, 559–594.

Transparency International. (2009). *Transparency in reporting on anti-corruption – A report of corporate practices TRAC*. Transparency International.

Transparency International UK. (2019). *At Your Service. Investigating how UK businesses and institutions help corrupt individuals and regimes launder their money and reputations*. Transparency International UK.

Transparency International UK. (2020). *Open business: Principles and guidance for anti-corruption corporate transparency*. Transparency International UK.

United Nations Development Programme (UNDP). (2008). *Asia Pacific human development report: Tackling corruption, transforming lives – Accelerating human development in Asia and the Pacific*. Delhi: Macmillan India.

UNGC. (2008). *Corporate citizenship in the world economy: UNGC*. UNGC.

UNGC. (2013). *A guide for anti-corruption risk assessment*. UNGC.

UNGC/GRI. (2007). *Making the connection: The GRI guidelines and the UNGC communication on progress*. UNGC.

UNGC/GRI. (2013). *Making the connection: Using the GRI G4 guidelines to communicate progress on the UN global compact principles*. UNGC/GRI.

UNGC/TI. (2009). *Reporting guidance on the 10th principle against corruption*. UNGC/TI.

United Nations. (2019). *Sustainable development goal 16: Focus on public institutions, World Public Sector Report 2019*. United Nations.

United States Agency of International Development (USAID). (2005). *Anticorruption strategy*. USAID.

Weber, S. (2019). *Evaluation of transparency international's transparency in corporate reporting (TRAC) tool*. HUMBOLDT-VIADRINA Governance Platform.

WEF. (2020). *Measuring stakeholder capitalism – Towards common metrics and consistent reporting of sustainable value creation*. WEF.

Wilkinson, P. (2006). Reporting on countering corruption. In B. Errath (Ed.), *Business against corruption: Case stories and examples* (pp. 96–107). United Nations GC Office.

Wilkinson, P. (2015). *Wise counsel or dark arts? Principles and guidance for responsible corporate political engagement*. Transparency International UK.

Chapter 6
Corporate Tax Behaviour

Abstract In this chapter, the relation between the tax behaviour of corporations and CSR is explored. The negative consequences of corporate tax avoidance and evasion are emphasised, namely those affecting nations and corporations. The argument that the pernicious social consequences of the generalised use of certain tax minimization strategies by corporations make their tax behaviour a matter of business assumption of social responsibilities is presented. Responsible tax behaviour is analysed as a CSR issue and is presented as an integral part of any corporation's social responsibility. The issue of how some CSR-related instruments deal with tax behaviour is addressed. The importance of responsible tax CSR policies and the reporting thereof is outlined as a basis for an effective fight against tax evasion and avoidance.

Keywords Corporate social responsibility · SR-related instruments · Responsible tax behaviour · Tax evasion · Tax avoidance · Tax mitigation · Tax transparency

6.1 The Role of Corporate Taxation in Modern Societies

The roles most commonly attributed to taxation are those of serving as a fundamental source of funding for the provision of goods and services by the state and promoting income and wealth redistribution. For example, in the case of Portugal, these two roles are enshrined in the Constitution of the Portuguese Republic, in its Article 103 (1), which states that "the fiscal system shall aim to satisfy the financial needs of the state and of other public bodies and to ensure a just distribution of income and wealth". Dietsch (2015, pp. 12–13) refers to these two central functions of taxation and adds a third, that of help stabilising the business cycle.

Also referring to the former two roles in their discussion of the "what are taxes for?" question, Avi-Yonah (2006, 2011) and Duff (2008) add a third, namely that of regulating social and economic behaviour. In the case of corporate taxation, this role concerns taxation being used to influence the behaviour of private sector agents by encouraging (subsidising) activities considered desirable and discouraging (penalising) those that are considered undesirable (Avi-Yonah, 2006, 2011). From

M. Castelo Branco, *Corporate Social Responsibility, the Fight Against Corruption and Tax Behaviour*, CSR, Sustainability, Ethics & Governance,
https://doi.org/10.1007/978-3-662-63735-7_6

this perspective, corporate taxation is also a way for the state to intervene directly in the business of corporations, and in this capacity, as an instrument of regulation, being "an important element in managing the delicate balance between business, society, and the state" (Avi-Yonah, 2004, p. 1255).

Leaving aside, for a moment, the specific case of corporate taxation, albeit the cases addressed in this and the following paragraph have strong implications for corporations, one of the most important examples of this role of regulating social and economic behaviour one can offer today is the so-called carbon tax (Avi-Yonah, 2011; Avi-Yonah & Uhlmann, 2009). According to the IMF (2019, p. 7), the most promising climate change mitigation economic policy instruments are those that enable carbon pricing, such as the carbon tax and the emissions trading systems. Later in this report, the IMF asserts that "the economic efficiency costs of carbon taxes are considerably lower than those of other mitigation instruments" (IMF, 2019, pp. 9–10). Contrasting and comparing these two instruments, Avi-Yonah (2011, p. 6) conclude that "at least in one important policy context, taxation is not just an acceptable vehicle for regulation, but the regulatory technique that is preferred by most commentators". And this researcher has not considered one issue that I deem extremely relevant when comparing the two instruments, that of fraud and corruption. One commentator that draws our attention to this aspect is William Nordhaus, who, for his contributions to the economic analysis of climate change, was awarded the 2018 *Sveriges Riksbank* Prize in Economic Sciences in Memory of Alfred Nobel (the so-called Nobel Prize in Economics) (shared with Paul Romer). In a book with the title "Climate Casino", this economist draws attention to the fact that, because they "create valuable assets in the form of tradable permissions", emissions trading systems are more susceptible to corruption, while a carbon tax, because it "it does not create artificial scarcities, monopolies, or rents", gives less room for such a phenomenon to occur (Nordhaus, 2013, p. 355).

There is one other, albeit less positive, example of this third role of taxation, that of tax competition, namely between countries. Many countries try to attract and maintain investors and residents which they deem as valuable, tailoring their tax policies to the needs of these agents (Dagan, 2018). As put by Dagan (2018, p. 6), such competition "gradually turns the tax policy decision-making process on its head", and the state is "increasingly functioning as a recruiter of investments and residents across the globe". Dietsch (2015, p. 2) goes as far as contending that tax competition "has become one of the principal policy variables employed by governments to shore up the 'competitiveness' of their economy—to attract capital and the jobs, as well as the economic growth this capital brings in its wake".

However, this tax competition has consequences. The OECD (2020) offers evidence pertaining to the generalised decline of statutory corporate tax rates. In this document, the OECD presents evidence of a significant change in the distribution of such rates between 2000 and 2020. Whereas in 2000, 68 of 109 jurisdictions in the OECD database presented corporate tax rates equal to or above 30%, only 21 jurisdictions were in these conditions in 2020. Regarding the average statutory tax rate, it has declined from 28% in 2000 to 20.6% in 2020. Avi-Yonah (2008, 2014) offers two reasons for this decline: the tax behaviour of corporations, which increasingly attempt to aggressively minimise their tax burden; and the growing tax competition between jurisdictions.

Fjeldstad et al. (2017, p. 47–48) refer to such decline as being in part a consequence of corporations and business interests' pressures to drive governments to offer lower tax levels to particular corporations or entire industries. These researchers also refer to the direct role played by corporations in driving such tax competition between jurisdictions, pointing to the numerous examples of corporations that have threatened to relocate their activities in other countries. Fjeldstad et al. (2017, p. 49) also draw attention to the consequences of the decline in corporate tax revenue. It may be compensated via increases in the tax burdens of consumers and employees, but it may also lead to cutting expenses and the provisioning of fewer or lower quality social services or attempts at attracting corporations by way of less stringent regulations pertaining to areas such as working conditions. Either way, as these researchers conclude, "unregulated tax competition may lead to a race to the bottom, not only in terms of tax levels but also in areas such as health, security and labour rights" (ibid.).

This third role of taxation can be looked at in a different way. Nowadays, as a result of the rise of large multinational corporations, which has led to a substantial weakening of the regulatory power of the state, an important justification for corporate taxation is its importance as a way for the state, in its capacity as the representative of the citizens (people), to limit the excessive accumulation of power in the hands of corporate managers (Avi-Yonah, 2004). From this perspective, corporate taxation has both a "limiting function" and a "regulatory function", with the former relating to directly limiting the rate of wealth accumulation by corporations and the latter relating to the provision of incentives and disincentives to particular activities deemed beneficial or detrimental to society as a whole (ibid.).

6.2 Corporate Tax Behaviour

Hanlon and Heitzman (2010, p. 137) refer to a continuum of tax planning strategies in which "something like municipal bond investments are at one end (lower explicit tax, perfectly legal)", while "terms such as 'noncompliance,' 'evasion,' 'aggressiveness,' and 'sheltering' would be closer to the other end". According to these researchers, "a tax planning activity or a tax strategy could be anywhere along the continuum depending upon how aggressive the activity is in reducing taxes" (ibid.).

For the sake of simplicity, I will use in what follows a different conceptualisation of the continuum of corporate tax strategies. I will refer to a "tax burden minimisation continuum", along which one can place the strategies used by corporations to minimise their tax burden. Referring to this same continuum, Loretz et al.

Using tax provisions in the spirit of the law	Rearrange international flows to avoid repatriation taxes	Reallocate the tax base to a lower-tax country	Reduce the tax base via a double deduction of double non-taxation	Illegal measures, e.g. non-disclosure of income
Tax mitigation	Tax avoidance			Tax evasion

Aggressiveness of corporate tax behaviour

Fig. 6.1 Tax burden minimisation continuum. Source: Adapted from Loretz et al. (2018, p. 23)

(2018) use the term "continuum of tax aggressiveness" and Onu et al. (2019) the term "compliance/non-compliance continuum".[1]

Following Choudhury and Petrin (2019), I will refer to three types of strategies: tax mitigation, tax avoidance,[2] and tax evasion. Albeit referring to a continuum, I find it important to note that the distinction between tax evasion and the other strategies is one of nature and not of degree since, unlike the other strategies, tax evasion is illegal. Tax mitigation may be thought of as the more legitimate and less aggressive or abusive of the two legal strategies. Given that in both cases there is compliance with the law, the main difference between tax mitigation and tax avoidance seems to pertain to the intention to go against (in the case of avoidance) or not (in the case of mitigation) the purpose or spirit of the law.

Considering the "tax burden minimisation continuum" (Fig. 6.1), tax planning can be thought of as the most legitimate of tax minimisation strategies. The other strategies range from illegal tax evasion to legal, though less legitimate than tax mitigation, tax avoidance. Establishing sharp boundaries between these strategies is a difficult task, as they extend along a continuum regarding which it is difficult to determine exactly where points distinguishing between the different types of strategies are. As asserted by Loretz et al. (2018, p. 23), "while it is theoretically possible to draw a line between acceptable tax planning and aggressive tax planning, the boundaries will in reality be somewhat blurred".

Tax mitigation can be understood as strategic behaviour designed to reduce the tax burden, increase profitability and increase value for the shareholders, without this

[1]Hasseldine and Morris (2018, p. 434) criticize the utilization of such a visual representation, which they do not find helpful, on the grounds that "at the very least it conceals, through an appeal to a visual representation which claims explanatory power, the difficulties that exist in any attempt to identify the characteristics that tax-related behaviour which is accepted as being legal but unacceptable possesses". Albeit acknowledging the validity of Hasseldine and Morris's arguments, given the introductory character of this book, I will use such a visual representation because I find it extremely useful as a visual aid to the text. Moreover, I agree with Loretz et al.'s (2018, p. 23) argument that its use "highlights the difficulties of defining sharp boundaries" regarding the aggressiveness of corporate tax behaviour.

[2]Loretz et al. (2018, p. 22) consider the terms "tax avoidance" and "aggressive tax planning" as describing the same behaviour and use them interchangeably. I prefer to use the term "tax avoidance".

happening at the expense of society as a whole. It is "clearly in the spirit of the law" and includes practices such as "claiming tax credits or using loss carry forwards" (Loretz et al., 2018, p. 23). Tax mitigation corresponds to that which Hardeck and Hertl (2014) call responsible corporate tax strategies. According to these researchers, corporations that use these latter strategies comply with the purpose of the law and refrain from pursuing all legal possibilities at their hand to minimise their tax burden. They go as far as contending that such corporations "intend to pay their *fair share* of taxes to ensure that the government is adequately financed" (p. 311). An example of such a strategy would be to respond to tax incentives offered by legislators to encourage certain activities.

Given that in both cases there is compliance with the legislation, the main difference between tax mitigation and tax avoidance appears to lie in whether or not the intention is to contravene the purpose or spirit of the law. In a very recent paper by the UK's HM Revenue and Customs, a distinction between the two tax burden minimisation strategies is made in a similar fashion (HM Treasury & HM Revenue & Customs, 2019): unlike tax avoidance, which is tantamount to circumventing the rules of the tax system to obtain tax advantages not intended by the legislature, tax mitigation involves taking advantage of tax reliefs for purposes for which they were intended. UNCTAD (2020, p. 5) also offers a similar view: "Tax evasion involves breaking the law, whereas tax avoidance involves the exploitation of national and international tax rules to gain advantages not intended by countries when they were adopted".

It would be possible to present the rationale of tax avoidance as being that of reducing the tax burden "at any price by exploiting loopholes, weaknesses or ambiguities in the law (i.e. movement of funds, construction of fictious or shell companies)" (Onu et al., 2019, p. 3). Tax avoidance refers to practices to which Hardeck and Hertl (2014, p. 310) refer to as aggressive corporate tax strategies and define as "corporate efforts to minimize tax liabilities by all legal means possible".

Probably the most widely known tool used by multinational corporations to engage in tax avoidance is profit shifting (Choudhury & Petrin, 2019). Among the many channels allowing to shift profits from high-tax jurisdictions to low- or no-tax jurisdictions through which multinational corporations aggressively minimise their tax burden, three are usually recognised in the literature (Janský & Palanský, 2019): strategic transfer pricing, debt shifting, and the location of intangible assets. Alluding more or less to these same channels, on which they focus their analysis, Loretz et al. (2018) refer to the two latter, on the basis of the main mechanism at work, as tax planning or income shifting through interest payments and tax planning or income shifting via royalty payments.

In a very recent report, the UNCTAD (2020) gives some prominence to the following methods:

1. Manipulation of the prices of goods and services charged internally within a group, with affiliates from high-tax countries importing them at high prices from those in low-tax countries.

2. Intragroup financing, with affiliates in high-tax jurisdictions borrowing from affiliates in low-tax ones.
3. Holding intangibles and intellectual property in tax havens and charging affiliates service fees for the use of such assets.

Other channels used include taking advantage of unintended opportunities for avoiding taxes provided by bilateral tax treaties via differences in clauses and concessions contained in them (UNCTAD, 2020).

A pedagogical illustration of the use of transfer pricing to minimise the tax burden that I find very interesting is offered by Fonseca-Statter (2011, p. 155), which I have slightly adapted in what follows. This researcher uses the example of a multinational corporation that exports from Portugal to the US bottles of port wine under the following condition: the selling price per unit is 3 €; the unit production cost is 2 €. Each bottle is sold for 12 € in the USA. Assuming that the corporation pays corporate income tax of 25 cents per bottle in Portugal and the equivalent of 2.7 € in the USA, the total tax payable per bottle is 2.95 €. In order to minimise the tax burden, the company decides to open a subsidiary in some tax haven where the tax is only 5%. Although the bottles are shipped directly from Portugal to the USA, the Portuguese subsidiary now bills the exports to the subsidiary in the tax haven, which bills the bottles to the US subsidiary at 10 € per bottle. As a result of this change, the company now pays tax at 25 cents in Portugal, 35 cents in the tax haven and 60 cents in the USA, i.e. 1.20 € in total, instead of 2.95 €.

The so-called Double Irish Dutch Sandwich has been one of the tax minimisation strategies most addressed in the literature (e.g. Choudhury & Petrin, 2019; Fonseca, 2020; Hansen, 2018; Jones et al., 2018; Mann et al., 2019; Munisami, 2018; Stewart, 2018; Zucman, 2014). The notoriety of this tax avoidance strategy is arguably related to having been used by corporations such as Apple, Facebook, Google, and Microsoft. A relatively recent report by the Fair Tax Mark (2019), a tax transparency group advocating for ethical tax policies, accused these four corporations of having used this or similar strategies. Fonseca (2020, p. 12) emphasises the notoriety of Google tax avoidance strategies by mentioning the use of the term "Google tax" to refer to anti-avoidance provisions passed in the United Kingdom and Australia.

Put it simply, the Double Irish Dutch Sandwich "involves the transfer of profits between subsidiaries in Ireland and the Netherlands with tax havens in the Caribbean as the typical final destination" (Damgaard et al., 2019, p. 12). The IMF (2018, p. 42) presented it as follows:

> Prior to 2015, the Irish definition of tax residence depended on the place of a company's effective management rather than incorporation. An MNE could therefore establish two subsidiaries in Ireland: an operating company that was both incorporated and tax-resident in Ireland, and an IP holding company that was incorporated in Ireland but tax-resident in a jurisdiction with extremely low or no corporate income tax. The operating company would receive income from sales throughout the region, but offset almost all of it with royalty payments to a related subsidiary in the Netherlands, which attracted no withholding tax. The Dutch company in turn distributed these payments to the "Irish" IP holding company as royalties. Dutch income tax was levied only on a small spread in the royalty rates, and there was no Dutch withholding tax on the payment of royalties under Dutch domestic law. From

a U.S. perspective, however, the income still appeared to be in Ireland, because the three entities would be combined into one Irish corporation through "check the box" elections. The 2015 change in Ireland's definition of tax residence to encompass all entities that are either incorporated or effectively managed in Ireland precluded these structures; however, existing structures were grandfathered through the end of 2020.

Strategies such as this are associated with the so-called phantom foreign direct investment (FDI). Damgaard et al. (2019) offer an interesting analysis of this phenomenon, on which what follows is based. To put it mildly, it is surprising that such a small country as Luxembourg is the host of as much FDI as the USA and much more than China. In truth, most of this FDI is "phantom in nature", that is, is "investment that pass through empty corporate shells", which have "no real business activities" (p. 12). What these shells do is "carry out holding activities, conduct intrafirm financing, or manage intangible assets—often to minimize multinationals' global tax bill" (ibid.). Luxembourg is not the only tax haven playing such a role. This country and the Netherlands are hosts of almost half of the world's phantom FDI. Among the ten economies that, together, host over 85% of phantom FDI, one can also find Switzerland and Ireland. Regarding this latter country, Damgaard et al. (2019, p. 13) note the astounding growth of Ireland's GDP by about 26% in 2015, in the wake of the relocation of intellectual property rights to Ireland by some multinational corporations.

Tax evasion is one of the strategies that corporations use to minimise their tax burden. It is, however, an illegitimate strategy, given its illegal nature. Its difference from tax avoidance, which is legal, is one of nature rather than degree, as mentioned above. Tax evasion involves deliberately not declaring or accounting for property or events (HM Treasury & HM Revenue & Customs, 2019). Prominent examples of tax evasion are not declaring income for tax purposes, false accounting or false invoicing (Jenkins & Newell, 2013).

Be that as it may, there is a great concern of citizens around the world regarding unacceptable tax behaviour (Edelman, 2017). Such concern is surely related to the number and media coverage of tax leak scandals that have occurred in the last decade (Table 6.1). Probably the most well-known of such recent scandals is the so-called Panama Papers. According to Fair Tax Mark (2020, p. 9), "within days of publication, protesters hit the streets, politicians resigned, police raided offices and prosecutors launched investigations".

6.3 Consequences of Irresponsible Corporate Tax Behaviour

Some of the better known consequences of tax avoidance and tax evasion by corporations worldwide are well evidenced by the following statement of OECD (2013, p. 5): "Base erosion constitutes a serious risk to tax revenues, tax sovereignty and tax fairness for OECD member countries and non-members alike. While there are many ways in which domestic tax bases can be eroded, a significant source of

Table 6.1 Timeline of tax leaks scandals

Offshore Leaks	April 2013	2.5mn records from 170 countries
Lux Leaks	November 2014	28,000 documents from PwC Luxembourg
Swiss Leaks	February 2015	60,000 files from HSBC Switzerland
Panama Papers	April 2016	11.5mn files from law firm Mossack Fonseca
Bahamas Leaks	September 2016	1.5mn documents from the Bahamas Corporate Registry
Paradise Papers	November 2017	13.4mn files from offshore law firm Appleby
Mauritius Leaks	July 2019	200,000 records from Mauritius office of law firm Conyers Dill & Pearman
Luanda Leaks	January 2020	Business practices of Isabel dos Santos and Angolan losses

Source: Fair Tax Mark (2020, p. 10)

base erosion is profit shifting." Consequences of irresponsible tax behaviour on tax bases have what some call "macroeconomic and societal risk", given that they have as a consequence decreases in public investment or decreased support for social provisioning programmes, which, in turn, have deleterious consequences in terms of economic growth and long-term investment returns (PRI, 2015, p. 10).

Because "the private sector is far from monolithic", it is also worthy of mention something that is not always acknowledged: "small businesses suffer more than most from the unlevel playing field created by multinationals' tax avoidance and the self-serving lobbying of their professional services firms" (Cobham, 2018).

Notwithstanding, the consequences of irresponsible tax behaviour go well beyond those mentioned above. Using the expression "negative externalities of tax avoidance" to refer to a number of deleterious consequences of such practice, including that of robbing "the public of revenue to support public goods, including infrastructure, education, and national defense", already mentioned above, Chaffee and Davis-Nozemack (2017, p. 1440) add three less direct and conspicuous consequences. First, that of undermining the functioning of the regulatory system. Second, that of forcing the establishment of a monitoring system that is more rigorous and costly by undermining the much-needed trust between corporations and those who regulate them. Third, that of undermining the business culture required for an organisation to be ethical. Fourth, given that such kind of practices requires obfuscation, they "can infect the morale, ethics, and culture of other parts of the firm" (ibid.).

Referring to these same consequences and relating irresponsible tax behaviour to the erosion of public commons, Bird and Davis-Nozemack (2018, p. 1021) offer a powerful look at why corporate tax avoidance can be seen as a sustainability problem by linking such a practice to the impairment of at least three commons "upon which efficient and fair relationships are based". Such an argument can obviously be extended to the case of tax evasion. Their argument goes as follows:

> Tax avoidance erodes the public commons by depriving elected governments of resources necessary to deliver shared public services for the benefit of all of society, including firms. Tax avoidance also weakens the regulatory commons. The work of tax avoidance experts corrodes trust between regulator and regulated and creates the need for increasingly complex regulatory language that imposes transaction costs on all firms. Tax avoidance also impairs the culture of the firm itself. Firms that aggressively avoid tax payments are at risk of fostering a culture with reduced respect for rules. (ibid.)

While the consequences of irresponsible corporate tax behaviour are also felt in developed countries, they are particularly damaging in developing countries. Global Financial Integrity (GFI) estimated that the volume of illicit financial flows related to crime, corruption, and tax evasion that flowed out of developing countries in 2011 amounted to USD 946.7 billion (GFI, 2013). Further, this organisation estimated that between 2002 and 2011, the total of such flows was USD 5.9 trillion (ibid.). In a previous report by the same organisation (GFI, 2010), it was recognised that despite the attention paid to the phenomenon of corruption, it was related to only about 3% of illicit financial flows (ibid.). Flows generated through criminal activities (drug trafficking, smuggling, etc.) would account for about 30–35% of the total. The largest share of such flows, between 60% and 65%, would be related to tax evasion (ibid.). It is not expected that there has been much change since then. In the most recent Global Financial Integrity report on illicit financial flows to and from developing countries (GFI, 2019), potential trade misinvoicing, which "is accomplished by misstating the value or volume of an export or import on a customs invoice" (p. xi), is mentioned as "primary means for illicitly shifting funds between developing and advanced countries" (p. x). Over the period 2006–2015, such practice has amounted to between 19% and 24% of developing country trade, on average (ibid.).

In this regard, Palan et al. (2010, p. 174) acknowledge that, "as is often the case with tax havens, the least important factor in terms of aggregate flows—corruption—has gained the greatest media attention. The most significant, transfer pricing, has attracted the least attention." These authors also do not fail to express surprise that many of the countries considered to be among the least corrupt according to Transparency International's CPI are countries where many of the proceeds of corruption are deposited, such as Switzerland or Luxembourg.

It is not only the minimisation of the tax burden through illegal methods that has pernicious consequences. Such tax minimisation through legal methods is also harmful. In Zambia, for example, Associated British Foods, a UK food multinational, is said to have deprived Zambia of some USD 17.7 million since 2007 through legal tactics used by its subsidiary Zambia Sugar Plc to avoid paying tax (Actionaid, 2013). This means that, in a country where one-third of child deaths were related to malnutrition, the transactions of just one multinational were estimated to have deprived the public coffers of a sum around 14 times greater than the aid provided by the United Kingdom to combat hunger and food insecurity in the same period (ibid.).

In addition to the macro-level detrimental consequences mentioned above, both in developed and developing countries, tax evasion and avoidance also cause risks and damages to corporations. In many situations, the costs of irresponsible tax behaviour translate into reduced profits for corporations, which means that the self-interest of a corporation can motivate the integration of CSR into its tax strategy. From this perspective, the issue of ethics and transparency in tax behaviour can, in many situations, be viewed as a form of strategic CSR, i.e. as a kind of investment from which corporations benefit. Five reasons justifying the integration of CSR into tax strategy have been put forward (van Eijsden, 2013, p. 59):

1. The cost for the business community as a whole resulting from the increasing scale and complexity of legislation created to address irresponsible tax behaviour.
2. Reputational risks for a corporation derived from the potential erosion of its position with its stakeholders as a result of adverse publicity.
3. Risks associated with litigation should the corporation's tax strategy be challenged by tax authorities or loss of access to public procurement contracts as a result of unacceptable tax behaviour.
4. Cash flow risks where irresponsible tax behaviour reduces confidence in future returns due to uncertainty over tax liabilities.
5. Investor confidence in accounting numbers may be affected due to the existence of potential tax effects.

Evidence regarding some of these consequences has been presented by Kepler Cheuvreux (2014, p. 9) in the form of a table (Table 6.2). Among such damages, Fisher (2014) emphasises those pertaining to corporate reputation and adds the additional one pertaining to the encouragement of other "subversive" practices by management. Regarding reputational effects, corporations whose success is heavily dependent on their reputations are very likely to discard tax avoidance schemes in favour of tax behaviours that attract less public scrutiny (ibid.). Opportunistic behaviour by managers is also a concern for tax authorities as well as for shareholders. The latter may well suspect that managers who are willing to cheat the state will also be willing to cheat the shareholders (ibid.).

Regarding the reputational risk of irresponsible tax behaviour, Kepler Cheuvreux (2014, p. 11) refers to the 2013 Best Global Brands Report, which mentioned tax associated with reputational risk in at least four of the corporations (Apple, Amazon, Goldman, and Starbucks) (Table 6.3). This report also included a mention associated with a positive reputational impact (Citi). Based on this information, Kepler Cheuvreux (2014, p. 11) noted "an increasing trend for tax to be a reputational factor where until recently it was considered a non-issue in branding terms".

Notwithstanding, regarding the reputational risks and based on an empirical illustration, Baudot et al. (2020) suggest that to some corporations tax behaviour may not have broad reputational effects, at least of such a magnitude that would entail changes in their behaviour. They put forward an interesting explanation for why some corporations may be less vulnerable to reputational risks associated with

Table 6.2 The rise of tax minimisation impacts on business

Type	Impacts	Examples
Costs	Settlements in tax disputes, i.e. transfer pricing	GSK USD3.4bn (US), AstraZeneca (USD1.1bn & GBP550m in UK), Vodafone (UK GBP1.25bn)
	Tax authority investigations from transfer pricing/cross border M&A	Novo Nordisk (Denmark USD1bn disputed), Vodafone, SAB Miller, AT&T, Shell (India)
	Delays to M&A/asset freezes and seizure	Nokia factory in India in handset IP tax dispute
	Criminal penalties	Credit Suisse USD2.8bn settlement and guilty plea for criminal charges of aiding US tax avoidance
	Bail money deposits required in disputes	UBS loses appeal for EUR1.1bn bail request in French courts for allegedly assisting French client tax avoidance
	Financial pressure on tax minimisation dependant business	Entire European offshore wealth management business unlikely to recover prior margin levels
	Increased legal and compliance costs	All the above examples
	Potential exclusion from public contracts due to tax evasion convictions	Regulation exists, i.e. for EU procurement, current levels of poor enforcement could increase in the long term
	EC investigations into unfair "fiscal state aid"	EC fiscal state aid investigations into Ireland and Netherlands may require repayments from companies with special tax agreements—so far Apple, Starbucks, Fiat potentially noted
	Suspension of key projects	First Quantum/Glencore suspends Zambia copper projects after government withholds USD tax refunds (200 m USD for Glencore)
Financial	Earnings volatility as a result of tax dispute/controversies	AstraZeneca
	Low-quality earnings	Various
	Short-term price impacts of regulatory changes	Shire/AstraZeneca 5% + drops Sept 2014 on new tax inversion regulation from US
	Requirement for organisational restructuring (i.e. of location and alignment of subsidiaries) as stricter tax haven legislation is introduced	Various
	Licence to operate—boycotts and public protests	Vodafone/Starbucks/Amazon UK
Reputational	Negative associations from impacts from televised senate parliamentary hearings on tax avoidance	Starbucks & Barclays (UK), Apple (US)
	Brand impact on entire bank from tax minimisation dependant business	Barclays tax avoidance units, European offshore wealth management sector

Source: Kepler Cheuvreux (2014, p. 9)

Table 6.3 Tax issues can affect mainstream evaluations of Brand Value

	Brand Value Impact	Total Brand Value USDm	Extract from Best Global Brands report (2013)
Apple	Negative	98,316	Apples' reputation has taken a few hits this past year... a US Senate hearing examining the company's "highly questionable" tax minimisation strategies
Amazon	Negative	23,620	The issue of tax avoidance in the UK demonstrates that Amazon's expansion plans must be checked with responsibility and prudence, or it faces risks to its brand reputation
Goldman	Negative	8536	Continuing to wrestle with negative public sentiment, the brand has been criticised for leveraging tax policy loopholes in The Volker Rule
Citi	Positive	7973	The brand has its "Citi for Cities" initiative: A prime example is its "e-payment gateway" in Mumbai to improve the tax collection and receipt process
Starbucks	Negative	4399	In the hot seat over corporate taxes in the UK, it remains to be seen whether this will have a long-term impact on the brand

Source: PRI (2015, p. 10)

irresponsible tax behaviour having to do with their celebrity status. Such status "creates path dependent and uneven effects in social evaluation and reputation for firms that engage in the same behaviors" (p. 210). Moreover, it may give a corporation "the license to engage in behaviors that stakeholders may find objectionable if such behaviors were committed by non-celebrity firms" (ibid.).

Whichever view of CSR one adheres to, be it the broader view according to which CSR encompasses legal responsibilities or the narrower view that limits CSR to voluntary initiatives, business practices that transgress the law always amount to socially irresponsible courses of action. However, this may only be so straightforward when we consider only the tax evader. When we consider the case of the tax planner assisting the evader, things are not so clear cut (Dietsch, 2011, p. 346). Consider the case of a bank operating in a tax haven that allows accounts to be opened without asking for personal information, which would allow the legality of the financial activity in question to be assessed (ibid.). Although some suggest that the obligation to obtain the relevant information can be considered a social responsibility of the tax planner (ibid.), this is debatable. Notwithstanding, any steps taken by a corporation to mitigate the detrimental effects resulting from third party tax avoidance on the welfare of society would presumably correspond to a socially responsible course of action (Williams, 2007).

6.4 Responsible Tax Behaviour Within the Framework of Corporate Social Responsibility

6.4.1 CSR and Responsible Tax Behaviour

In June 2013, the leaders of the G8 nations signed a declaration (known as the Lough Erne Declaration) recognising the importance of automatic information sharing by tax authorities around the world to "tackle the scourge of tax fraud", as stated in the first of its ten points. In the second point, it adds the need to change the rules that allow companies to transfer profits to avoid paying tax and for multinationals to report to the tax authorities on the taxes they pay and where they pay them.

It can be argued that this statement is the result of a debate that has become increasingly participatory and noisy and seems to have culminated in international policymakers making ethics and transparency in tax behaviour one of their priorities. Over 15 years ago, Christensen and Murphy (2004, p. 37) expressed their astonishment that tax minimisation, particularly when pursued through strategies whose primary or sole purpose is tax avoidance, was considered to be "one of the prime duties" of a corporation's directors towards its shareholders. They found it even more curious that the CSR debate, which had until the moment in which these researchers were writing focused on "virtually every other area of corporate engagement with broader society", had only begun to "question companies in the area where their corporate citizenship is most tangible and most important—the payment of taxes" (ibid.). Such astonishment was shared by Desai and Dharmapala (2006, p. 4), who emphasised the fact that tax payments by corporations are their "largest and most obvious contributions" to stakeholders other than shareholders and employees.

Already a little over 10 years ago, two practitioners, partners of PricewaterhouseCoopers, went as far as claiming that "paying tax into public finances is clearly part of how business contributes to society" (Scheiwiller & Symons, 2010, p. 28). Taxes, they stress, "provide essential public revenues for governments to meet economic and social objectives" (ibid.). These professionals view the payment of taxes by corporations as "clearly part of the economic dimension" of how corporations impact the community and how they "contribute to the creation of prosperity and to stability" (ibid.). Interestingly enough, they also emphasise as other aspects of this economic dimension the creation of jobs and employment, as well as the generation of business for suppliers. By the late 2000s, this economic dimension of corporate responsibility was, compared to the social and environmental dimensions, arguably at a lower level of development and was commonly assimilated to financial performance (Landolf & Symons, 2008).

Early in the decade that has just ended, Shaxson (2011) considered tax behaviour to be the missing element in the CSR debate. Over 7 years ago, KPMG (2013) addressed this issue and listed a number of factors that it considered to have been determining factors for this topic to have emerged as one of the priorities in the international political debate. In addition to the new economic realities faced by governments following the 2008 global crisis, the increased media focus on corporate taxation issues, the internationalisation of businesses, the ever-increasing use of the internet in the sale of goods and services, the role played by the growing importance of the CSR movement is also emphasised (ibid.). KPMG considered at the time that the new wave of CSR would be based on anti-corruption and taxation issues (ibid.).

One of the possible explanations for the lack of attention regarding tax behaviour within CSR debates until relatively recently could be its less sensationalist and attention-capturing nature when compared to environmental and human rights-related abuses (Fisher, 2014). Notwithstanding, the media attention that has been devoted in the last decade to the tax behaviour of companies such as Apple, Google, Amazon, or Starbucks may be associated with the recent coming to the fore of responsible tax behaviour (ibid.).

Dowling (2014) offered a different explanation for the apparent lack of interest in corporate tax behaviour among scholars in earlier CSR debates, that of the importance of stakeholder theory in informing their perspectives. For this researcher, given that the main proponents of this theory considered employees, customers, and investors as corporations' main stakeholders, tax behaviour did not emerge as a fundamental topic in the debate insofar as the direct impacts of irresponsible tax behaviour on these agents are not negative. Dowling argued that if the state where to shift from the background to the foreground in the approach to CSR based on stakeholder theory, issues such as that of tax evasion would attract greater scrutiny.

I do not find it difficult to agree with the arguments presented by Shaxson (2011) in favour of the need to rethink the concept of corporate responsibility. For this author, corporations are granted immense privileges, such as those of limited liability and the possibility of being treated as artificial legal entities. While the former allows investors to cap their losses and shift debts to other members of society when things go wrong, the latter allows companies to locate themselves in different jurisdictions regardless of where they actually do business. The obligations that corporations were originally given in exchange for such privileges, transparency about their businesses and the payment of taxes have been progressively undermined, notably by the offshore system. While privileges have been preserved and even augmented, obligations have languished. Shaxson concluded that it is necessary to immediately include tax behaviour in debates on corporate responsibilities. This seems to have happened to some extent during the last decade.

Notwithstanding, certain views of CSR allow one to look at a corporation's aggressive tax planning strategy either as positive or negative from a CSR point of view. If one accepts the influential view of CSR proposed by Archie Carroll, one of the pioneers in the development of the CSR concept, as encompassing the economic, legal, ethical, and philanthropic responsibilities that a company has towards its various stakeholders (Carroll, 1991), it is not difficult to establish relationships between corporate tax behaviour and CSR, albeit conflicting ones. From an economic point of view, reductions in a corporation's tax burden lead to improvements in its profitability and increases in the wealth of its shareholders. From society's point of view, taxes are essential to fund the state's social programmes (such as those pertaining to education, health care, or public transportation, among many others). Whatever the case may be, the association of tax payments by corporations with CSR is mostly addressed on the basis of considerations regarding their implications for the wider community from the point of view of their role as a source of financing the provision of public goods (Lanis & Richardson, 2012). Based on Carroll's (1991) view, Hardeck and Hertl (2014, p. 313) argue that: because it leads to a lower tax burden, tax avoidance is consistent with the economic responsibility, and because it is legal tax behaviour, it is in line with the legal responsibility. Notwithstanding, because it leads to "reductions in national tax revenue and a redistribution of the tax burden to fall on smaller companies and households", such behaviour conflicts with the ethical responsibility (p. 322). Gribnau (2015) and Gribnau and Jallai (2017) offer relatively similar perspectives.

For Gribnau and Jallai (2017, p. 82), although CSR "might not be a quick solution to diminish tax planning practices", at least it opens "a door for discussion in order to establish what are legitimate or acceptable tax planning practices". These researchers claim that "morality is inherent in taxation" and this "does not do away with the simple fact that taxes are also an expense" (p. 77). For these researchers, although taxpayers (including corporations) "have a right to structure their affairs to achieve a favorable tax treatment within the limits set by law", they "should balance this right with the duty of fair play towards society and thereby impose restraints on themselves in taking advantage of the inevitable imperfections of the legal system" (p. 84). I subscribe to this view, but I do not consider that it can be explored using Carroll's pyramid of corporate responsibilities. One of the reasons for this is that in Carroll's view, the legal responsibility seems to be restricted to the "letter" of the law, whereas the "spirit" of the law seems to be reserved for the ethical responsibility (Geva, 2008). I do not consider this to be an adequate framework.

I consider that a concentric circles type of approach to CSR (Geva, 2008), as presented in Chap. 3, is more appropriate to the examination of tax behaviour as a CSR issue. According to such a view of CSR, one cannot think of economic responsibilities without considering their legal and ethical aspects. Tax payments are primarily an economic responsibility, but they are also an expression of how the corporation relates to all its members, not only the state. I consider that there is an overarching ethical concern no matter what type of human activities one is considering. This idea is consistent with the views of the economy, ethics, development, and CSR presented in the first part of this book. How the corporation relates to the state should be driven by ethical considerations, like all other relations, with employees, suppliers, and so on and so forth.

In Chap. 3, I have presented four theories of the corporation: the artificial entity theory; the aggregate theory; the real entity theory; and the collaboration theory. Whatever the view one takes regarding which one is the most appropriate theory, a corporation carrying out strategies designed solely to minimise its tax burden cannot be considered as consistent with CSR (Avi-Yonah, 2014; Munisami, 2018). From the point of view of the artificial entity theory, this kind of behaviour undermines the connection between the state and the corporation it has created. From the point of view of the real entity theory, such behaviour is as unacceptable as it would be for any individual citizen. From the point of view of the aggregate theory, tax behaviour of this kind deprives the state of the means necessary to perform the increased obligations that result from not allowing CSR activities. The result would be that neither corporations nor the state would be able to address the numerous existing social problems (Knuutinen, 2014, p. 50), many of them caused by corporations' activities. As Avi-Yonah (2014, p. 26) puts it regarding this latter theory:

> The basic problem is that, under the aggregate view, most CSR activities are illegitimate. This necessarily means that the responsibilities devolve upon the state, which is supposed to use its legitimate taxing function to raise money to fulfill these obligations. But if all corporations engage in strategic tax behavior, the state probably will not be able to raise sufficient money to fulfill its exclusive social responsibility functions.

If one takes a collaboration theory point of view, tax avoidance becomes impermissible (Chaffee, 2019). Given that "collaborators in business ventures owe each other a duty of good faith, and the contractual nature of the corporation carries with it a duty of a good faith as well", the idea that depriving the state of revenue through tax avoidance is permissible cannot hold (p. 162). Amounting, by definition, to a violation of the spirit of the law, tax avoidance "is an affront to the collaboration that forms the foundation of the corporate form because it frustrates one of the government's purposes for entering the collaboration (i.e. gaining revenue)" (ibid.).

Chaffee (2019) explores four scenarios to examine when a corporation has the obligation not to engage in a tax avoidance strategy. The first pertains to a situation in which such a strategy implies costs greater than the benefits it entails. The second is that of such a strategy being cost-neutral. The third scenario concerns a setting in which it is uncertain whether the strategy will result in a loss or a gain for the corporation. In the fourth scenario, it is certain that the strategy will lead to a financial benefit to the corporation. Grounded on collaboration theory, which he has created, Chaffee (2019, p. 157) claims that "tax avoidance should be avoided in all circumstances", including those in which there is a clear benefit accruing to the corporation. Explaining why this is so, Chaffe argues that:

> A for-profit corporation unsurprisingly exists to make a profit, and under collaboration theory, the government and the individuals organizing, operating, and owning the corporation have created the entity for purposes of economic development and economic gain. When corporate managers engage in tax avoidance, they frustrate one of the government's main reasons for collaborating within the corporate form (i.e. to procure funds via taxation for purposes of maintaining and improving the state) (ibid.).

Chaffee (2019) also raises the question of why tax avoidance is not permissible, while tax mitigation is. After all, in both cases, the government is deprived of revenue. The difference pertains to tax mitigation amounting to tax minimisation conducted within both the spirit and the letter of the law, whereas the case is not the same with tax avoidance. Remember that the latter is not in accordance with the spirit of the law. As argued by Chaffee (2019, p. 161), albeit tax avoidance amounts to a violation only of the spirit of the law, "one would have a difficult time arguing that the deal struck with the government was that those individuals could be abusive to the laws and regulations of the government".

institutions, and, in particular, regarding profits made, taxes paid, and subsidies received, is essential for regaining the trust of citizens of the Union in the financial sector", and that "mandatory reporting in that area can therefore be seen as an important element of the corporate responsibility of institutions towards stakeholders and society". Financial institutions are required to "disclose annually, specifying, by Member State and by third country in which it has an establishment", annual information on a consolidated basis on: the name(s), nature of activities and geographical location; turnover; number of employees on a full-time equivalent basis; profit or loss before tax; tax on profit or loss; public subsidies received.

Not least because it has been discussed on the 25th February 2021 by EU member states' ministers (Ryding, 2021), it is also important to mention the "proposal for a Directive of the European Parliament and of the Council amending Directive 2013/34/EU with regard to disclosure of income tax information by certain undertakings and branches" (European Commission, 2016). If this proposal were to be approved, multinational groups exceeding the revenue threshold of EUR 750 million would be required to "draw up and publish a report on income tax information on an annual basis" (art. 48b). Regarding the content of such a report, the proposal mentions that it should include information on items such as the nature of the activities, number of employees, net turnover, profit or loss before income tax, tax accrued and tax paid, amount of accumulated earnings (art. 48c):

A comparison of the tax reporting requirements of these two directives and the proposal of directive is presented in Table 6.4.

The OECD Guidelines for Multinational Enterprises

The final chapter (Chap. 9) of the OECD Guidelines for MNEs is on "Taxation". It is composed of the following two paragraphs:

> 1. It is important that enterprises contribute to the public finances of host countries by making timely payment of their tax liabilities. In particular, enterprises should comply with both the letter and spirit of the tax laws and regulations of the countries in which they operate. Complying with the spirit of the law means discerning and following the intention of the legislature. It does not require an enterprise to make payment in excess of the amount legally required pursuant to such an interpretation. Tax compliance includes such measures as providing to the relevant authorities timely information that is relevant or required by law for purposes of the correct determination of taxes to be assessed in connection with their operations and conforming transfer pricing practices to the arm's length principle.
>
> 2. Enterprises should treat tax governance and tax compliance as important elements of their oversight and broader risk management systems. In particular, corporate boards should adopt tax risk management strategies to ensure that the financial, regulatory and reputational risks associated with taxation are fully identified and evaluated.

The United Nations Global Compact

The UNGC does not make any reference to tax behaviour.

Table 6.4 Tax reporting requirements in EU legal instruments

		Proposal for a directive	Capital requirements directive	New accounting directive
Basic information	Entity name		X	
	Activities	X	X	
	Geographical location/tax jurisdiction		X	X
	Project name			X
	Receiving government			X
Financial data	Revenue	X	X	
	Profit or loss before tax	X	X	
	Tangible assets other than cash or cash equivalents			
	Stated capital			
	Accumulated earnings	X		
Tax data	Income taxes paid	X	X	X
	Income tax charge	X		
Other data	Public subsidies received		X	
	Dividends			X
	Royalties			X
	Licence fees, rental fees, and entry fees			X
	Signature, discovery, and production bonuses			X
	Production entitlements			X
	Payment for infrastructure improvements			X
People data	Number of employees	X	X	

Source: PRI (2018, p. 21)

ISO 26000

ISO 26000 only briefly mentions taxation in issue 5, "Wealth and income creation", within the core subject "community involvement and development": "An organization should fulfil its tax responsibilities and provide authorities with the necessary information to correctly determine taxes due".

The GRI Standards

Even before the publication of the most recent GRI Standard, GRI 207: Tax 2019 (GRI, 2020), some researchers went as far as claiming that the GRI was "already at the forefront of considering taxation as part of an overall sustainability analysis" (Bird & Davis-Nozemack, 2018, p. 1018). In effect, since its 2002 version, the GRI guidelines include indicators pertaining to tax behaviour (Table 6.5).

Table 6.5 Tax-related indicators in GRI Guidelines

G2	G3/G3.1	G4
EC8. Total sum of taxes of all types paid broken down by country	EC1. Direct economic value generated and distributed, including revenues, operating costs, employee compensation, donations and other community investments, retained earnings, and payments to capital providers and governments[a]	**EC1. Direct economic value generated and distributed** (1) Direct economic value generated and distributed (EVG&D) on an accruals basis including the basic components for the organisation's global operations as listed below. If data is presented on a cash basis, report the justification for this decision and report the basic components as listed below: (a) Direct economic value generated: (i) Revenues. (b) Economic value distributed: (i) Operating costs. (ii) Employee wages and benefits. (iii) Payments to providers of capital. (iv) Payments to government (by country). (v) Community investments. (c) Economic value retained (calculated as "direct economic value generated" less "Economic value distributed"). (2) To better assess local economic impacts, report EVG&D separately at country, regional, or market levels, where significant. Report the criteria used for defining significance
EC9. Subsidies received broken down by country or region. This refers to grants, tax relief, and other types of financial benefits that do not represent a transaction of goods and services	EC4—Significant financial assistance received from government.	**EC4. Financial assistance received from government** (1) Total monetary value of financial assistance received by the organisation from governments during the reporting period, including, as a minimum: (a) Tax relief and tax credits (b) Subsidies (c) Investment grants, research and development grants, and other relevant types of grants (d) Awards (e) Royalty holidays (f) Financial assistance from Export Credit Agencies (ECAs) (g) Financial incentives (h) Other financial benefits received or receivable from any government for any operation (2) Report the information above by country (3) Report whether, and the extent to which, the government is present in the shareholding structure

[a]Payments to government: All company taxes (corporate, income, property, etc.) and related penalties paid at the international, national, and local levels. This figure should not include deferred taxes because they may not be paid. For organisations operating in more than one country, report taxes paid by country. The organisation should report which definition of segmentation has been used

Table 6.6 Tax-related reporting requirements in GRI 201: Economic performance.

Disclosure 201-1—Direct economic value generated and distributed	Disclosure 201-4—Financial assistance received from government
(a) Direct economic value generated and distributed (EVG&D) on an accruals basis, including the basic components for the organisation's global operations as listed below. If data are presented on a cash basis, report the justification for this decision in addition to reporting the following basic components: (i) Direct economic value generated: revenues; (ii) Economic value distributed: operating costs, employee wages and benefits, payments to providers of capital, payments to government by country, and community investments; (iii) Economic value retained: "direct economic value generated" less "economic value distributed" (b) Where significant, report EVG&D separately at country, regional, or market levels, and the criteria used for defining significance	(a) Total monetary value of financial assistance received by the organisation from any government during the reporting period, including: (i) tax relief and tax credits; (ii) subsidies; (iii) Investment grants, research and development grants, and other relevant types of grant; (iv) awards; (v) royalty holidays; (vi) financial assistance from Export Credit Agencies (ECAs); (vii) Financial incentives; (viii) Other financial benefits received or receivable from any government for any operation (b) The information in 201-4-a by country (c) Whether, and the extent to which, any government is present in the shareholding structure

A substantial change in the approach occurred with the GRI Standards (GRI, 2020). Besides the information related to the direct economic value generated and distributed, demanded since the G3 iteration, now demanded in GRI 201: Economic Performance (Table 6.6), in 2019, the GRI standard GRI 207: Tax was added to the other standards.

Müller et al. (2020) establish the connection between the GRI 207 standard and the two instruments of tax transparency mentioned above: similar to the UK tax strategy report, GRI's tax standard demand qualitative information on the approach to tax and tax governance; similar to public country-by-country reporting, GRI 207 demand a comprehensive list of tax-related items on a country-by-country basis (Table 6.7).

Country-by-country reporting is defined in GRI 207: Tax as involving "the reporting of financial, economic, and tax-related information for each jurisdiction in which an organization operates. This indicates the organization's scale of activity and the contribution it makes through tax in these jurisdictions."

Other Relevant Instruments

As in the case of the fight against corruption, regarding tax behaviour, I consider it relevant to also address the Extractive Industries Transparency Initiative (EITI), the World Economic Forum's (WEF) "Measuring Stakeholder Capitalism—Towards Common Metrics and Consistent Reporting of Sustainable Value Creation"

Table 6.7 GRI 207: Tax reporting requirements and recommendations

Management approach disclosures	Topic-specific disclosure
Disclosure 207–1—Approach to tax (a) A description of the approach to tax, including: (i) whether the organisation has a tax strategy and, if so, a link to this strategy if publicly available; (ii) the governance body or executive-level position within the organisation that formally reviews and approves the tax strategy, and the frequency of this review; (iii) the approach to regulatory compliance; (iv). how the approach to tax is linked to the business and sustainable development strategies of the organisation	*Disclosure 207–4—Country-by-country reporting* (a) All tax jurisdictions where the entities included in the organisation's audited consolidated financial statements, or in the financial information filed on public record, are resident for tax purposes (b) For each tax jurisdiction reported in Disclosure 207–4-a: (i) Names of the resident entities; (ii) Primary activities of the organisation; (iii) Number of employees, and the basis of calculation of this number; (iv) Revenues from third-party sales; (v) Revenues from intragroup transactions with other tax jurisdictions; (vi) Profit/loss before tax; (vii) Tangible assets other than cash and cash equivalents; (viii) Corporate income tax paid on a cash basis; (ix) Corporate income tax accrued on profit/loss; (x) Reasons for the difference between corporate income tax accrued on profit/loss and the tax due if the statutory tax rate is applied to profit/loss before tax (c) The time period covered by the information reported in Disclosure 207–4 *In addition to these reporting requirements, the following reporting recommendations are put forward:* The reporting organisation should report the following additional information for each tax jurisdiction reported in Disclosure 207-4-a: 1. Total employee remuneration; 2. Taxes withheld and paid on behalf of employees; 3. Taxes collected from customers on behalf of a tax authority; 4. Industry-related and other taxes or payments to governments; 5. Significant uncertain tax positions; 6. Balance of intra-company debt held by entities in the tax jurisdiction.
Disclosure 207-2—Tax governance, control, and risk management (a) A description of the tax governance and control framework, including: (i) the governance body or executive-level position within the organisation accountable for compliance with the tax strategy; (ii) how the approach to tax is embedded within the organisation; (iii) the approach to tax risks, including how risks are identified, managed, and monitored; (iv) how compliance with the tax governance and control framework is evaluated (b) A description of the mechanisms for reporting concerns about unethical or unlawful behaviour and the organisation's integrity in relation to tax (c) A description of the assurance process for disclosures on tax and, if applicable, a reference to the assurance report, statement, or opinion	
Disclosure 207-3 *Stakeholder engagement and management of concerns related to tax* (a) A description of the approach to stakeholder engagement and management of stakeholder concerns related to tax, including: (i) the approach to engagement with tax authorities; (ii) the approach to public policy advocacy on tax; (iii) the processes for collecting and considering the views and concerns of stakeholders, including external stakeholders.	

(in collaboration with Deloitte, EY, KPMG, and PwC), and the Transparency International UK's (2020) "Principles and guidance for anti-corruption corporate transparency". Besides these instruments, I also consider worthy of note, albeit a brief one, B Team's Responsible Tax Principles, the Australian Taxation Office's Voluntary Tax Transparency Code, and Spain's Large Companies Forum's Code of Good Tax Practices.

As mentioned in the previous chapter, EITI is one of the most influential initiatives appealing to transparency as a strategy to combat corruption and tax evasion and avoidance. Although Aaronson (2011, p. 52) refers to the EITI as an initiative aimed at curbing corruption and improving government, this initiative is often associated with tax issues and country-by-country reporting (e.g. Chatzivgeri et al., 2017; Cobham et al., 2018; Fjeldstad et al., 2017; PRI, 2018; STAR Collective, 2020; Wójcik, 2015). As previously mentioned, amidst other demands, the EITI demands that governments disclose information on the income received from corporations in the oil, gas, and mining sectors and that corporations disclose payments to the governments of the countries in which they operate.

Transparency International UK (2020) includes country-by-country reporting in the five key areas that it considers of high risk of corporate corruption (already mentioned in the introductory chapter). Besides such type of reporting, it considers beneficial ownership reporting, organisational structure reporting, and corporate political engagement reporting. Regarding "country-by-country reporting transparency", Transparency International UK (2020, p. 39) proposes the following two principles:

1. The company should publicly disclose the nature of work, the countries of operations and the countries of incorporation of its fully consolidated subsidiaries and non-fully consolidated holdings.
2. The company should publicly disclose country-by-country breakdowns of its payments to governments.

Regarding the first principle, Transparency International UK emphasises the importance of disclosures detailing the nature of the activities of a corporation's subsidiaries, the countries of operation, and the countries of incorporation to enable those interested in appraising whether the corporation's operations have been established for legitimate purposes. Concerning the second principle, Transparency International UK mentions that the disclosures it proposes include "revenue/sales, capital expenditure, pre-tax income, income tax and community contributions in all countries in which the company operates" (ibid.). It also stresses the importance for a corporation to publicly disclose "the contributions that it makes beyond taxation of its corporate income, including sales taxes, payroll taxes, customs duties, property taxes and environmental levies" (ibid.).

WEF (2020) includes the aspect of responsible tax behaviour under the themes "employment and wealth generation" and "community and social vitality" of the Prosperity pillar. It proposes two core metrics and disclosures, economic contribution and total tax paid, and two expanded metrics and disclosure, additional tax

Table 6.8 Tax-related metrics and disclosures in WEF (2020)

Theme	Core metrics and disclosures	Expanded metrics and disclosures
Employment and wealth generation	*Economic contribution* 1. Direct economic value generated and distributed (EVG&D), on an accruals basis, covering the basic components for the organisation's global operations, ideally split out by: (a) Revenues (b) Operating costs (c) Employee wages and benefits (d) Payments to providers of capital (e) Payments to government (f) Community investment 2. Financial assistance received from the government: total monetary value of financial assistance received by the organisation from any government during the reporting period	
Community and social vitality	*Total tax paid* The total global tax borne by the company, including corporate income taxes, property taxes, non-creditable VAT and other sales taxes, employer-paid payroll taxes, and other taxes that constitute costs to the company, by category of taxes	*Additional tax remitted* The total additional global tax collected by the company on behalf of other taxpayers, including VAT and employee-related taxes that are remitted by the company on behalf of customers or employees, by category of taxes
		Total tax paid by country for significant locations Total tax paid and, if reported, additional tax remitted, by country for significant locations

remitted and total tax paid by country for significant locations (Table 6.8). As one can see, these metrics and disclosures are strongly influenced by the GRI Standards. Unfortunately, the WEF (2020) decided not to be as demanding regarding country-by-country reporting.

Other relevant initiatives that I will mention only in passing are the Australian transparency code released by the Australian Board of Taxation in May 2016 (De la Cuesta-González & Pardo, 2019, p. 2173; Gribnau et al., 2018) and the Code of Good Tax Practices (Código de Buenas Prácticas Tributarias) of the Spain's Large Companies Forum (Foro de Grandes Empresas) which comprises the Spanish National Tax Agency (Agencia Tributaria) and twenty-seven of the country's largest companies, endorsed in July 2010 (Gribnau et al., 2018).

Another initiative worthy of mention is the Responsible Tax Principles proposed by B Team (2018). B Team is "a not-for-profit initiative formed by a global group of business leaders to catalyse a better way of doing business, for the wellbeing of people and the planet". Its Responsible Tax Principles include seven principles on: (1) accountability and governance; (2) compliance; (3) business structure; (4) relationships with authorities; (5) seeking and accepting tax incentives; (6) supporting effective tax systems; (7) transparency.

Regarding principles 1–6, Cobham et al. (2018) asserts that while their "mood music" is ok, "commitments to comply with the law, or existing positions on beneficial ownership transparency, don't exactly move the needle". But, for him, it is concerning principle 7 "where it's really disappointing". This researcher voices his disappointment regarding B Team's principle on transparency as follows: "and crucially on transparency, what is immediately clear is that the B Team principle—despite making most of the right noises—stops well short of requiring any kind of consistent reporting" (ibid.). This criticism is not without merit given B Team's principles lack of specification regarding how country-level information should be reported. According to B Team (2019, p. 1), such lack of specification "was intentional, recognising that practice in this area is still emerging".

6.4.3 Some Evidence on Tax Transparency

As in the case of the fight against corruption, in what follows, I will present the main results regarding tax transparency of Transparency International's TRAC studies and the Alliance for Corporate Transparency's study on the implementation of the EU NFRD (Alliance for Corporate Transparency, 2020). I will also refer to evidence provided in PRI (2018) regarding tax transparency of fifty multinational corporations in the healthcare and information technology sectors.

Alliance for Corporate Transparency (2020, p. 66) provides evidence on tax transparency. Results suggest a "relatively low coverage of reporting on tax-related policies and commitments from a country-by-country perspective" (ibid.). While 54.8% of the corporations refer to their tax policies, only 15.7% report on specific policies and procedures. The analysis of the issues addressed in such policies revealed that only a minority expressed commitment to pay taxes where profits are generated (19.3%) and commitment against tax avoidance strategies (14.8%) (Table 6.9). Less than 9% provide information on income taxes paid disaggregated for country. One can see that, when compared to anti-corruption reporting, tax behaviour reporting is even less developed.

Regarding country-by-country reporting, the TRAC tool assesses such reporting based on five questions pertaining to the disclosure of revenues and some expenses on a country-by-country basis: revenue/sales; capital expenditure; pre-tax income; income tax; community contributions.

In Table 6.10, a summary of the average country-by-country reporting score as reported in the TRAC reports is provided, both those prepared by TI regarding global

Table 6.9 Specific aspects addressed in tax transparency

Aspects	%
Policies and outcomes—issues addressed	
Commitment to pay taxes where the profits generated	19.3
Commitment against tax avoidance strategies	14.8
Provision of effective tax rate	64.6
Profits before taxes	
KPI disaggregated for country	7.2
Income taxes paid	
KPI disaggregated for country	8.9

Source: Based on Alliance for Corporate Transparency (2020, p. 66)

Table 6.10 Country-by-country reporting (CbC) in TRAC reports

Year	No. Assessed corporations	Average results CbC (%)
Panel A—Global		
2012	105	4
2014	124	6
Panel B—EMM		
2013	100	9
2016	100	9
Panel C—Local		
Belgium (2016)	27	12
Brazil (2018)	110	3
Chile (2014)	19	19
Denmark (2016)	30	3
Italy (2013)	15	6
Hungary (2013)	50	30
Kuwait (2013)	4	49
Lithuania (2017)	49	34
Netherlands (2019)[a]	29	15
Norway (2013)	50	8
Russia (2018)	200	4
South Africa (2020)[a]	100	36
South Korea (2016)	50	1
Sweden (2013)	20	40
Si Lanka (2020)[a]	50	33
Turkey (2015)	100	8
Ukraine (2016)	100	37
Vietnam (2018)	45	0

Source: Adapted from Weber (2019, p. 77)
[a]Information directly obtained in the TRAC report

multinational corporations and those prepared by TI national chapters. Table 6.10 is based on Weber (2019, p. 77). Regarding the information presented by this researcher, I only include in this table information based on the most recent TI national chapter TRAC report in the cases in which two or more reports have been published (Belgium, Denmark, Lithuania, and South Africa). Given that some reports have been published subsequently to the publication of Weber's study, I have included the new information based on these new reports. As one can see, levels of country-by-country reporting are very low.

The United Nations Principles for Responsible Investment (PRI) commissioned a research on corporate income tax disclosure of fifty healthcare and technology multinational corporations, whose results are reported in PRI (2018). Among the reasons adduced by PRI to explain the selection of these sectors, the following are included: corporations in these sectors have been known for presenting the highest tax gap when compared to other sectors; they also have been exposed to high media scrutiny and government inquiries; they present levels of tax transparency that can be depicted as poor. The main findings of this research are presented in Table 6.11.

PRI (2018, p. 10) emphasises the following findings pertaining to tax policy: almost 30% of the corporations in the sample published a tax policy; only about 20% of them published more comprehensive tax policies and strategy documents; around 25% provided a meaningful narrative on tax risks; only just a little over 15% of the corporations examined described how their tax structures and strategies align taxes paid with economic value generated; only around 25% of them (mainly those bound by the UK Finance Act) reported on their relationship with tax authorities; none of the corporations disclosed in detail their lobbying and advocacy activities on tax or the channels they used to influence public policy. Regarding governance and risk management, PRI (2018, p. 10) stressed the following results: over 20% of the corporations surveyed stated that the board is responsible for tax governance; only around 10% of them referred to staff training to manage tax positions appropriately or to meet regulatory requirements; none of the corporations in the sample explicitly referred to their whistleblowing procedures relating to their tax policy. Finally, regarding performance, PRI (2018, p. 11) emphasised the following results of the research: about 50% of the corporations analysed clarified why their effective tax rate (ETR) increased or decreased when compared to previous years; none of the corporations described tax strategies that may be contributing to changes in uncertain tax benefits (UTBs); only around 5% provided some level of information on debt arrangements with subsidiaries; over 35% of the corporation (particularly those having to comply with SEC reporting requirements) reported on tax incentives; none of the corporations published a country-by-country report; over 70% reported on disputes with tax authorities.

All the evidence presented in this chapter points to very low levels of tax transparency and the provision of very superficial information on the topic.

Table 6.11 Overview of tax disclosure practices of fifty selected healthcare and technology multinational corporations

	<10% of companies	10–25% of companies	Over 25% of companies
Policy	• Address broader economic impacts in their tax policy and outline alignment with business and sustainability strategy • Discuss advocacy and lobbying • Indicate membership in trade associations active on tax policy • Have a policy signed by a board-level representative • Reference impact on overall profitability in their tax policy • Discuss stakeholders' trust, values or explain if engagement has impacted policy • Commit to transparent tax-related reporting • Describe relationship with other stakeholders including assessing perceptions regarding the spirit of tax laws	• Describe relationships with tax authorities • State risk appetite • State link between where profit is booked and commercial activity • Provide overview of general tax structures and strategies	• Publish a tax policy
Governance and risk management	• Provide evidence that the board discusses ramifications on reputation • Provide information on whistleblowing channels • Reference third-party standards and guidelines • Provide examples of acceptable and unacceptable practices, and how tax havens are used, if applicable • Indicate that tax policy and strategy are reviewed at least annually	• Provide a statement on tax governance and risk oversight • Disclose mechanisms to maintain compliance with the firm's tax policy • Describe the process to interpret the law and deal with ambiguity • Provide information on training and guidance	• Provide a narrative on major tax risks
Performance	• Disclose new tax strategies being employed leading to increases in UTBs • Disclose intra-company debt balances, name countries where intercompany debt is held and disclose average interest rate paid on intercompany debt • Publish country-level tax reporting • Explain key tax strategies employed in relation to ETR and use global weighted average in ETR reconciliation	• Potential regulatory changes related to tax strategies • Information on the expiration date of tax incentives	• ETR reconciliation • Statement on UTBs • List of subsidiaries • Current disputes with tax authorities • Information on financially material tax incentives

(continued)

Table 6.11 (continued)

	<10% of companies	10–25% of companies	Over 25% of companies
	• Provide commentary on the likelihood of non-renewal of incentives • Highlight investment requirements of each incentive		

Source: PRI (2018, p. 6)

References

Aaronson, S. A. (2011). Limited partnership: Business, Government, Civil Society, and the public in the Extractive Industries Transparency Initiative (EITI). *Public Administration and Development, 31*(1), 50–63.

ActionAid. (2013). *Sweet nothings: The human cost of a British sugar giant avoiding taxes in southern Africa*. ActionAid.

Alliance for Corporate Transparency. (2020). *Research Report 2019: An analysis of the sustainability reports of 1000 companies pursuant to the EU Non-Financial Reporting Directive*. Alliance for Corporate Transparency.

Avi-Yonah, R. S. (2004). Corporations, society, and the state: A defense of the corporate tax. *Virginia Law Review, 90*(5), 1193–1255.

Avi-Yonah, R. S. (2006). The three goals of taxation. *New York University Tax Law Review, 60*(2), 1–28.

Avi-Yonah, R. S. (2008). Corporate social responsibility and strategic tax behavior. In W. Schön (Ed.), *Tax and corporate governance* (pp. 183–198). Springer.

Avi-Yonah, R. S. (2011). Taxation as regulation: Carbon tax, health care tax, bank tax and other regulatory taxes. *Accounting, Economics, and Law, 1*(1), Artigo 6.

Avi-Yonah, R. S. (2014). Corporate taxation and corporate social responsibility. *New York University Journal of Law and Business, 11*(1), 1–29.

Avi-Yonah, R. S., & Uhlmann, D. M. (2009). Combating global climate change: Why a carbon tax is a better response to global warming than cap and trade. *Stanford Environmental Law Journal, 28*(3), 3–50.

B Team. (2018). *A new bar for responsible tax principles*. The B Team Responsible Tax Principles. B Team.

B Team. (2019). *Public tax reporting. Learning by doing and through dialogue*. Accessed February 18, 2021, from https://bteam.org/assets/reports/Public-Tax-Reporting-Learning-by-Doing-and-Through-Dialogue.pdf

Baudot, L., Johnson, J. A., Roberts, A., & Roberts, R. W. (2020). Is corporate tax aggressiveness a reputation threat? Corporate accountability, corporate social responsibility, and corporate tax behavior. *Journal of Business Ethics, 163*, 197–215.

Bird, R., & Davis-Nozemack, K. (2018). Tax avoidance as a sustainability problem. *Journal of Business Ethics, 151*(4), 1009–1025.

Carroll, A. (1991). The pyramid of corporate social responsibility: Toward the moral management of organizational stakeholders. *Business Horizons, 34*, 39–48.

Chaffee, E. C. (2019). Collaboration theory and corporate tax avoidance. *Washington and Lee Law Review, 76*, 93–162.

Chaffee, E. C., & Davis-Nozemack, K. (2017). Corporate tax avoidance and honoring the fiduciary duties owed to the corporation and its stockholders. *Boston College Law Review, 58*, 1425–1481.

Chatzivgeri, E., Chew, L., Crawford, L., Gordon, M., & Haslam, J. (2017). *Reports on payments to governments: A report on early developments and experiences, report for publish what you pay international secretariat and publish what you pay UK*. Robert Gordon University.

Chatzivgeri, E., Chew, L., Crawford, L., Gordon, M., & Haslam, J. (2020). Transparency and accountability for the global good? The UK's implementation of EU law requiring country-by-country reporting of payments to governments by extractives. *Critical Perspectives on Accounting, 67*, 102074.

Choudhury, B., & Petrin, M. (2019). *Corporate duties to the public*. Cambridge University Press.

Christensen, J., & Murphy, R. (2004). The social irresponsibility of corporate tax avoidance: Taking CSR to the bottom line. *Development, 47*(3), 37–44.

Cobham. (2018). *The B-Team: Lowering the bar for tax transparency?* Accessed February 18, 2021, from https://www.taxjustice.net/2018/02/16/b-team-lowering-bar-tax-transparency/

Cobham, A., Janský, P., & Meinzer, M. (2018). A half-century of resistance to corporate disclosure. *Transnational Corporations, 25*(3), 1–27.

Col, B., & Patel, S. (2019). Going to haven? Corporate social responsibility and tax avoidance. *Journal of Business Ethics, 154*(4), 1033–1050.

Dagan, T. (2018). *international tax policy: Between competition and cooperation*. Cambridge University Press.

Damgaard, J., Elkjaer, T., & Johannesen, N. (2019). The rise of phantom investments. *Finance & Development, 56*(3), 11–13.

Davis, A. K., Guenther, D. A., Krull, L. K., & Williams, B. M. (2016). Do socially responsible firms pay more taxes? *The Accounting Review, 91*(1), 47–68.

De la Cuesta-González, M., & Pardo, E. (2019). Corporate tax disclosure on a CSR basis: A new reporting framework in the post-BEPS era. *Accounting, Auditing and Accountability Journal, 32* (7), 2167–2192.

Desai, M., & Dharmapala, D. (2006). Corporate social responsibility and taxation: The missing link. *Leading Perspectives, 4*(57), 4–5.

Dietsch, P. (2011). Asking the fox to guard the henhouse. The tax planning industry and corporate social responsibility. *Ethical Perspectives, 18*(3), 341–354.

Dietsch, P. (2015). *Catching capital: The ethics of tax competition*. Oxford University Press.

Dowling, G. R. (2014). The curious case of corporate tax avoidance: Is it socially irresponsible? *Journal of Business Ethics, 124*, 173–184.

Duff, D. G. (2008). *Tax fairness and the tax mix*. Foundation for Law, Justice and Society.

Edelman. (2017). *2017 Edelman trust barometer - Global report*. Edelman.

European Commission. (2011). *Communication from the Commission to the European Parliament, the Council, the European Economic and Social Committee and the Committee of the Regions. A renewed EU strategy 2011–14 for Corporate Social Responsibility*. COM 2011(681) final.

European Commission. (2012). *Action plan to strengthen the fight against tax fraud and tax evasion*. COM (2012)722 final.

European Union. (2013a). *DIRECTIVE 2013/34/EU OF THE EUROPEAN PARLIAMENT AND OF THE COUNCIL of 26 June 2013 on the annual financial statements, consolidated financial statements and related reports of certain types of undertakings, amending Directive 2006/43/ EC of the European Parliament and of the Council and repealing Council Directives 78/660/ EEC and 83/349/EEC*.

European Union. (2013b). *DIRECTIVE 2013/36/EU OF THE EUROPEAN PARLIAMENT AND OF THE COUNCIL of 26 June 2013 on access to the activity of credit institutions and the prudential supervision of credit institutions and investment firms, amending Directive 2002/87/ EC and repealing Directives 2006/48/EC and 2006/49/EC*.

European Commission. (2016). *Proposal for a DIRECTIVE OF THE EUROPEAN PARLIAMENT AND OF THE COUNCIL amending Directive 2013/34/EU as regards disclosure of income tax information by certain undertakings and branches*.

European Union. (2014). Directive 2014/95/EU of the European Parliament and of the Council of 22 October 2014 amending Directive 2013/34/EU as regards disclosure of non-financial and

diversity information by certain large undertakings and groups. *Official Journal of the European Union*.
Fair Tax Mark. (2019). *The Silicon Six and their $100 billion global tax gap*. Fair Tax Mark.
Fair Tax Mark. (2020). *The essential elements of global corporate standards for responsible tax conduct (public consultation draft)*. Fair Tax Mark.
Fisher, J. M. (2014). Fairer shores: Tax havens, tax avoidance, and corporate social responsibility. *Boston University Law Review, 94*, 337–365.
Fjeldstad, O.-H., Jacobsen, S. K., Ringstad, P. H., & Ngowi, H. P. (Eds.). (2017). *Lifting the veil of secrecy: Perspectives on international taxation and capital flight from Africa*. Chr. Michelsen Institute.
Fonseca, J. (2020). ESG investing: How corporate tax avoidance affects corporate governance & ESG analysis. *Illinois Business Law Journal, 25*, 1–18.
Fonseca-Statter, G. (2011). *O Preço das Coisas. Conversas à volta de um café*. . . Página a Página.
Forstater, M. (2016). Publishing corporate tax strategies. *Tax Journal, 5*, 10–12.
Geva, A. (2008). Three models of corporate social responsibility: Interrelationships between theory, research, and practice. *Business and Society Review, 113*(1), 1–41.
Global Financial Integrity (GFI). (2010). *Illicit financial flows from Africa: Hidden resource for development*. Global Financial Integrity.
Global Financial Integrity (GFI). (2013). *Illicit financial flows from developing countries: 2002–2011*. Global Financial Integrity.
Global Financial Integrity (GFI). (2019). *Illicit financial flows to and from 148 developing countries: 2006–2015*. Global Financial Integrity.
GRI. (2020). *Consolidated set of GRI sustainability reporting standards 2020*. GRI.
Gribnau, H. (2015). Corporate social responsibility and tax planning: Not by rules alone. *Social and Legal Studies, 24*(2), 225–251.
Gribnau, H., & Jallai, A.-G. (2017). Good tax governance: A matter of moral responsibility and transparency. *Nordic Tax Journal, 1*, 70–88.
Gribnau, H., van der Enden, E., & Baisalbayeva, K. (2018). Codes of conduct as a means to manage ethical tax governance. *Intertax, 46*(5), 390–407.
Hanlon, M., & Heitzman, S. (2010). A review of tax research. *Journal of Accounting and Economics, 50*(2–3), 127–178.
Hansen, R. F. (2018). Taking more than they give: MNE tax privateering and apple's "ocean" income. *German Law Journal, 19*(4), 693–726.
Hardeck, I., & Hertl, R. (2014). Consumer reactions to corporate tax strategies: Effects on corporate reputation and purchasing behavior. *Journal of Business Ethics, 123*(2), 309–326.
Hasseldine, J., & Morris, G. (2018). Unacceptable tax behaviour and corporate responsibility. In N. Hashimzade & Y. Epifantseva (Eds.), (pp. 430–457). Routledge.
Hearson, M. (2019). Fair tax for development. In F. Carver (Ed.), *Sustainable development goals: Transforming our world* (p. 62). United Nations Association.
HM Treasury, & HM Revenue & Customs. (2019). *Tackling tax avoidance, evasion and other forms of non-compliance*. Accessed February 18, 2021, from https://assets.publishing.service.gov.uk/government/uploads/system/uploads/attachment_data/file/785551/tackling_tax_avoidance_evasion_and_other_forms_of_non-compliance_web.pdf
Hoi, C. K., Wu, Q., & Zhang, H. (2013). Is corporate social responsibility (CSR) associated with tax avoidance? Evidence from irresponsible CSR activities. *The Accounting Review, 88*(6), 2025–2059.
Huang, H. H., Sun, L., & Yu, T. R. (2017). Are socially responsible firms less likely to expatriate? An examination of corporate inversions. *The Journal of the American Taxation Association, 39*(2), 43–62.
Huseynov, F., & Klamm, B. K. (2012). Tax avoidance, tax management and corporate social responsibility. *Journal of Corporate Finance, 18*, 804–827.
International Monetary Fund (IMF). (2018). *The impact of international tax reforms on Ireland*. In IMF, Ireland: Selected issues, IMF Country Report No. 18/195, 18–44.

International Monetary Fund (IMF). (2019). *Fiscal monitor: How to mitigate climate change*. IMF.
Janský, P., & Palanský, M. (2019). Estimating the scale of profit shifting and tax revenue losses related to foreign direct investment. *International Tax and Public Finance, 26*(5), 1048–1103.
Jenkins, R., & Newell, P. (2013). CSR, tax and development. *Third World Quarterly, 34*(3), 378–396.
Jones, C., Temouri, Y., & Cobham, A. (2018). Tax haven networks and the role of the Big 4 accountancy firms. *Journal of World Business, 53*(2), 177–193.
Kepler Cheuvreux. (2014). *Tax me if you can: Game over–Turning Grey areas into red flags for investors*. Kepler Cheuvreux.
Kleizen, B. (2019). Victims of their own success abroad? Why the withdrawal of US transparency rules is hindered by diffusion to the EU and Canada. *Journal of European Public Policy, 26*(3), 446–467.
Knuutinen, R. (2014). Corporate social responsibility, taxation and aggressive tax planning. *Nordic Tax Journal, 2014*(1), 36–75.
Knuutinen, R., & Pietiläinen, M. (2017). Responsible investment: Taxes and paradoxes. *Nordic Tax Journal, 2017*(1), 135–150.
Kovermann, J., & Velte, P. (2021). CSR and tax avoidance: A review of empirical research. *Corporate Ownership and Control, 18*(2), 20–39.
KPMG. (2013). *A new era in international tax. Tax morality, transparency, base erosion and profit shifting*. KPMG International.
Landolf, U., & Symons, S. (2008). Applying corporate responsibility to tax. *International Tax Review, 44*, 6–13.
Landry, S., Deslandes, M., & Fortin, A. (2013). Tax aggressiveness, corporate social responsibility, and ownership structure. *Journal of Accounting, Ethics and Public Policy, 14*(3), 611–645.
Lanis, R., & Richardson, G. (2012). Corporate social responsibility and tax aggressiveness: An empirical analysis. *Journal of Accounting and Public Policy, 31*, 86–108.
Lanis, R., & Richardson, G. (2015). Is corporate social responsibility performance associated with tax avoidance? *Journal of Business Ethics, 127*(2), 439–457.
Lanis, R., & Richardson, G. (2018). Outside directors, corporate social responsibility performance, and corporate tax aggressiveness: An empirical analysis. *Journal of Accounting, Auditing and Finance, 33*(2), 228–251.
Loretz, S., Sellner, R., Brandl, M. B., Arachi, G., Bucci, V., van't Riet, M., & Aouragh, A. (2018). *Aggressive tax planning indicators*. Publications Office of the European Union.
Mann, R., Martin, F., & Butcher, B. (2019). Saving the planet by cutting corporate taxes: A comparative case study analysis. *Florida Tax Review, 23*, 238.
Mao, C. W. (2019). Effect of corporate social responsibility on corporate tax avoidance: Evidence from a matching approach. *Quality and Quantity, 53*(1), 49–67.
Mayberry, M. A., & Watson, L. (2021). Is corporate social responsibility related to corporate tax avoidance? Evidence from a natural experiment. *Journal of the American Taxation Association, 43*(1), 79–106.
Muller, A., & Kolk, A. (2015). Responsible tax as corporate social responsibility: The case of multinational enterprises and effective tax in India. *Business and Society, 54*(4), 435–463.
Müller, R., Spengel, C., & Vay, H. (2020). *On the determinants and effects of corporate tax transparency: Review of an emerging literature*. ZEW-Centre for European Economic Research Discussion Paper (20–063).
Munisami, K. (2018). The role of corporate social responsibility in solving the great corporate tax dodge. *Florida State University Business Review, 17*, 55–86.
Murphy, R. (2012). *Country-by-country reporting. Accounting for globalisation locally*. Report prepared for Tax Justice Network. Accessed March 02, 2021, from http://www.taxresearch.org.uk/Documents/CBC2012.pdf
Murphy, R. (2016). Country-by-country reporting. In T. Pogge & K. Mehta (Eds.), *Global tax fairness* (pp. 96–112). Oxford University Press.

Narotzki, D. (2016). Corporate social responsibility and taxation: The next step of the evolution. *Houston Business and Tax Law Journal, 16*, 167–207.
Narotzki, D. (2017). Corporate social responsibility and taxation: A chance to develop the theory. *Western New England Law Review, 39*, 539–556.
Nordhaus, W. D. (2013). *The climate casino: Risk, uncertainty, and economics for a warming world*. Yale University Press.
Oats, L., & Tuck, P. (2019). Corporate tax avoidance: Is tax transparency the solution? *Accounting and Business Research, 49*(5), 565–583.
OCDE. (2013). *Addressing base erosion and profit shifting*. OECD Publishing.
OECD. (2020). *corporate tax statistics* (2nd ed.). OECD.
Onu, D., Oats, L., Kirchler, E., & Hartmann, A. J. (2019). Gaming the system: An investigation of small business owners' attitudes to tax avoidance, tax planning, and tax evasion. *Games, 10*(4), 46.
Ortas, E., & Gallego-Álvarez, I. (2020). Bridging the gap between corporate social responsibility performance and tax aggressiveness. *Accounting, Auditing and Accountability Journal, 33*(4), 825–855.
Palan, R., Murphy, R., & Chavagneux, C. (2010). *Tax havens: How globalization really works*. Cornell University Press.
Preuss, L. (2010). Tax avoidance and corporate social responsibility: You can't do both, or can you? *Corporate Governance, 10*, 365–374.
Preuss, L. (2012). Responsibility in paradise? The adoption of CSR tools by companies domiciled in tax havens. *Journal of Business Ethics, 110*(1), 1–14.
Principles for Responsible Investment (PRI). (2015). *Engagement guidance on corporate tax responsibility: Why and how to engage with your investee companies*. The Principles for Responsible Investment (PRI).
Principles for Responsible Investment (PRI). (2018). *Evaluating and engaging on corporate tax transparency: An investor guide*. PRI.
Renouard, C., & Ezvan, C. (2018). Corporate social responsibility towards human development: A capabilities framework. *Business Ethics: A European Review, 27*(2), 144–155.
Ryding, T. (2021). *Eurodad reaction to EU ministers' discussion about public country by country reporting today*. Accessed March 05, 2021, from https://www.eurodad.org/eurodad_reaction_to_eu_ministers_discussion_about_public_country_by_country_reporting_today
Scheiwiller, T., & Symons, S. (2010). Corporate responsibility and paying tax. *OECD Observer, 276/277*, 27–28.
Shaxson, N. (2011). *Treasure Islands: Uncovering the damage of offshore banking and tax havens*. Palgrave Macmillan.
Sikka, P. (2010). Smoke and mirrors: Corporate social responsibility and tax avoidance. *Accounting Forum, 34*(3–4), 153–168.
STAR Collective. (2020). *Accounting and the mitigation of the resource curse: Exploring the efficacy of the EU law concerning reports on payments to governments in country-specific contexts across the EU*. Association for Accountancy & Business Affairs.
Stewart, J. (2018). MNE tax strategies and Ireland. *Critical Perspectives on International Business, 14*(4), 338–361.
Transparency International UK. (2020). *Open Business: Principles and Guidance for Anti-Corruption Corporate Transparency*. Transparency International UK.
UNCTAD. (2020). *Tackling illicit financial flows for sustainable development in Africa*. Geneva: United Nations Publications.
van Eijsden, A. (2013). The relationship between corporate responsibility and tax: Unknown and unloved. *EC Tax Review, 2013/1*, 56–61.
Weber, S. (2019). *Evaluation of transparency international's transparency in corporate reporting (TRAC) tool*. HUMBOLDT-VIADRINA Governance Platform.

WEF. (2020). *Measuring stakeholder capitalism – Towards common metrics and consistent reporting of sustainable value creation*. WEF.
Williams, D. F. (2007). *Tax and corporate social responsibility*. KPMG.
Wójcik, D. (2015). Accounting for globalization: Evaluating the potential effectiveness of country-by-country reporting. *Environment and Planning C, 33*(5), 1173–1189.
Zucman, G. (2014). Taxing across borders: Tracking personal wealth and corporate profits. *Journal of Economic Perspectives, 28*(4), 121–148.

Chapter 7
Final Remarks

Abstract This final chapter serves to emphasise the idea that one cannot address corporate corruption and irresponsible tax behaviour without also addressing a broad range of other practices that also pertain to the interface between politics and business, ranging from the revolving door phenomenon to lobbying. Such practices are inextricably linked with corruption and tax avoidance.

Keywords Corporate social responsibility · Corporate political activity · Fight against corruption · Institutional corruption · Responsible tax behaviour

7.1 Corruption, Taxation, and Corporate Political Activity

Jackie Chan expressed in 2012 the opinion that the US is the most corrupt country in the world. That statement was, as one might expect, widely publicised, and the actor was severely criticised for his supposed "anti-Americanism" (Fisher, 2013). However, a number of renowned intellectuals from the US have been producing similar statements. For example, in 2014, Joseph Stiglitz said that if India is a corrupt country, the US is a good competitor. In February 2016, in his blog, writing about whether the phenomenon of corruption is more serious in Brazil or in the US, Henry Mintzberg considered that, at least in one critical respect, it is not in Brazil that the situation is most serious (Mintzberg, 2016). According to Mintzberg, while in Brazil, corruption is criminal and can be prosecuted, in the US, it is legal, and its perpetrators do not suffer any kind of legal sanctions. In 2016, in an article published in The Guardian, Jeffrey Sachs (2016) suggested that to stop corruption, we should start with the US and the UK. This statement by Sachs should be read in the light of what this economist wrote in a 2011 article entitled "The Global Economy's Wave of Corporate Crime" (Sachs, 2011):

> The world is drowning in corporate fraud, and the problems are probably greatest in rich countries—those with supposedly 'good governance.' Poor-country governments probably accept more bribes and commit more offences, but it is rich countries that host the global

M. Castelo Branco, *Corporate Social Responsibility, the Fight Against Corruption and Tax Behaviour*, CSR, Sustainability, Ethics & Governance,
https://doi.org/10.1007/978-3-662-63735-7_7

companies that carry out the largest offences. Money talks, and it is corrupting politics and markets all over the world.

Stiglitz's and Mintzberg's statements should also be read in the light of this observation.

It is the existence of what is called by many "legal corruption" (e.g. Graycar & Monaghan, 2015) that leads renowned scholars like Mintzberg, Sachs, and Stiglitz to suggest that the key to mitigating the problem lies in combating it in developed countries. In these countries, corruption is associated with phenomena such as the financing of political parties and election campaigns, corporate political connections (such as the revolving door phenomenon) or lobbying. These corporate practices, among others, correspond to what is now called "corporate political activity".

There are numerous cases of former politicians pursuing their careers in the private sector. Examples involving leaders of the European Commission have multiplied over the years (Dialer & Richter, 2019). Two such cases have caused great controversy. One of the most recent, in July 2016, was the appointment of Durão Barroso (former European Commission President) as chairman and adviser at Goldman Sachs. Silva (2019, p. 278) refers to this case as "Barrosogate" and mentions the episode of Barroso having been exposed in February 2018 as continuing to hold "meetings with sitting Commissioners to discuss policy issues which were logged as lobby meetings with Goldman Sachs". The other case is that of Günter Verheugen, Commissioner for Enterprise and Industry between 2004 and 2010, who created the consultancy firm European Experience Company. The Royal Bank of Scotland acknowledges that they have hired the former commission "for his experience and contacts in European politics" (Oluwole, 2019, p. 298).

In the foreword to a 2016 OECD report on "Financing Democracy: Funding of Political Parties and Election Campaigns and the Risk of Policy Capture", Angel Gurría, OECD Secretary-General at the time, points out some of the consequences of the capture by private interests of public policymaking: "erosion of democratic governance, social cohesion, equal opportunities, as well as the decline of trust in democracy itself" (OECD, 2016, p. 3). He ends by asserting that "in democracies, public policy should never be for sale to the highest bidder" (p. 4).

At this point in the book, I deem it important to relate what has just been asserted to the recent Covid-19 pandemic. The number of news on the usage of the Covid-19 pandemic by multinational companies and business associations to pressure public decision-makers to take decisions to their advantage is staggering. For example, a recent report by Friends of the Earth with the telling title "Cashing in on COVID" (Ross, 2020), in which the case of US-based oil and gas companies and their trade associations during the first quarter of 2020 was analysed, provides evidence of the lobbying efforts and the large benefits obtained by these corporations from support resulting from policies to respond to the Covid-19 pandemic, including tax breaks and stimulus loans.

Multinational corporations and their associations also seemed to have used the Covid-19 pandemic to lobby to seek to counter or delay climate change policies. So much so that the leading organisation Carbon Market Watch felt the need to publish a briefing denouncing what they call "industry climate lobbying", with the title "Never Wasting a Crisis" (Carbon Market Watch, 2020). The briefing concludes that several attempts have been made to use the Covid-19 pandemic "as a pretext to weaken national, European and international climate legislation and the implementation of the EU Green Deal" (p. 10). According to the briefing, highly polluting industries have put pressure on policymakers to grant them exemptions "to serve their short-term economic interest and lock us into highly polluting and destructive fossil fuel based economies" (ibid.).

But this type of behaviour by these corporations is not new. For example, referring to the US case, Brulle (2018) begins by asserting that in the US "climate legislation has often been the focus of intense lobbying" (p. 289). This researcher considers that despite other factors explaining the failure to pass climate legislation, "lobbying is seen as an important influence on legislative outcomes" (p. 290). Brulle estimates that lobbying expenditure related to this type of legislation in the period 2000–2016 exceeded $2 billion. The most substantial share of this expenditure comes from sectors that produce and use fossil fuels, which is about 10 times greater than the share coming from environmental organisations and the non-renewable energy sector.

Equally important has been the funding of climate denial organisations by these corporations. Wilkinson (2015) considers this type of practice as indirect lobbying. For example, Grasso (2019) refers to Exxon Mobil's funding of 69 such organisations during the period 1998–2014. Also in the case of the US, Cory et al. (2021) present evidence that companies and industries that are characterised by CO_2-intensive emissions are more likely to join public efforts to oppose climate change action and policies and that this opposition extends to their suppliers and customers, who face costs arising from such action and policies transmitted via the supply chain. According to these researchers, efforts in the public sphere of this "expanded carbon coalition", as they call the coalition of corporations, associations, and other groups that publicly oppose public action and policy to reduce greenhouse gas emissions, "are significant, and they are matched by significant activity in lobbying" (p. 85).

Some researchers have even sought to estimate the social cost of lobbying over climate policy. In a pioneering study, Meng and Rode (2019) examined the extent to which lobbying around the "Waxman-Markey bill, the most prominent and promising US climate regulation to date," (p. 472) by large corporations has decreased the likelihood of its implementation. The results of the study led these researchers to conclude that lobbying against the bill was more effective than lobbying for it and that lobbying over the bill decreased the likelihood of passing it by 13 percentage points. Moreover, using a measure of the social cost of carbon and a forecast of the emissions that would have been avoided if the bill had been implemented, these authors estimated the social cost of such lobbying at US$60 billion.

All these practices and the loss of business legitimacy that is likely to ensue are certainly among the motivations for the recent initiative on responsible corporate climate change lobbying developed by AP7, the largest Swedish public pension fund, BNP Paribas Asset Management, and the Church of England Pensions Board, in partnership with Chronos Sustainability, to influence this type of lobbying, namely by creating a framework with the help of which such lobbying can be carried out responsibly.

Even if one has not an approach to corporate corruption as encompassing as the one proposed by Fleming and Zyglidopoulos (2009), presented in the introductory chapter, the connection between corruption and these corporate practices is not difficult to discern. In its Guide for Anti-Corruption Risk Assessment, referring to the manyfold forms of corruption, the UNGC (2013, pp. 12–13) mentions the revolving door phenomenon explicitly and considers political donations as a form of bribery. It also considers tax evasion as a form of corruption.

It is not possible to refer to tax minimisation without referring to corporate lobbying. Again, what is at stake is lobbying for regulations that are beneficial to business but harmful to society. Oxfam America (2017) provided evidence that during the period 2009–2015, the 50 largest corporations from the US spent about US$2.5 billion on lobbying, with around US$352 million spent in lobbying on tax issues alone. Meanwhile, over US$423 billion in tax breaks were received by these corporations, which means that they received an estimated US$1200 for every US$1 spent lobbying on tax issues. Fair Tax Mark (2019, p. 13) reveals telling information on the spending on lobbying activities by the so-called Silicon Six (Facebook, Apple, Amazon, Netflix, Google, and Microsoft). These corporations have collectively spent between 2015 and 2019 in the US over US$257 m. During this same period, taxation was the most raised topic in Microsoft and Apple lobbying activities, whereas in the cases of Amazon and Facebook it was, respectively, the second and the third.

At this point, it is also worthy of mention the participation of some governments in tax avoidance. Cobham et al. (2018, p. 8) refer to the LuxLeaks revelations of how Luxembourg has approved numerous secret low- or zero-tax deals that have been proposed by the big four accounting corporations of major multinationals and to the European Commission's State aid investigations revelations of Belgian and Irish States' substantial efforts to facilitate profit-shifting practices.

7.2 Institutional Corruption

Practices in which corporations engage leading to detrimental results for society, including corruption, tax evasion, and tax avoidance, lobbying for regulations that are beneficial to business, but harmful to society, maybe be thought of in the light of the concept of "institutional corruption". This concept of institutional corruption was developed by, among others, Lawrence Lessig (Amit et al., 2017; Lessig, 2013, 2015).

Lessig is an American academic, professor of law at Harvard University, and a political activist who became better known to the public for being a candidate for the Presidency of the USA in the 2016 elections. The motivation that Lessig presented to embark on such a journey was related to the importance he attached to the influence of "money" in politics. His main intention was to reduce such influence. For Lessig and his supporters, the US political system is rigged on behalf of the wealthiest and most powerful and ignores the interests of "normal" citizens. The influence of money on politics has meant that representative democracy has become so corrupt that only those who significantly finance political campaigns see their interests represented. This fundamental inequality influences how everything is handled, from climate change to reforms in the financial system.

At the basis of Lessig's proposals is the notion of "institutional corruption". This institutional perspective on corruption implies that the corruption of institutions and not just individuals is also addressed and reflected upon. Lessig acknowledges the problems of bribery and the influence of interest groups in decision-making by politicians (that is, the way in which such groups achieve favourable laws through their political contributions). Nevertheless, he also considers that saying that an institution is corrupt is not the same as saying that it is full of corrupt individuals (it may or may not be). In the case of an institution, to say that it has been corrupted is tantamount say that it does not work in order to achieve its purpose and that something has interfered with its ability to function as originally intended and to pursue its purpose.

For Lessig, despite being ethically respectable and decent people, politicians and lobbyists end up enmeshed in a system of mutual dependence in which money influences decision-making. This influence may not be direct, as shown by the example of members of the US Congress with few contributors. In these cases, the scarcity of resources leads them to rely on lobbyists to obtain relevant information or even write their proposals, depending more on their knowledge than on the money. Lessig considers that institutional corruption is confirmed when public trust decreases as a consequence of the collective perception that the institution and its leaders no longer behave in accordance with the general understanding of its purpose.

Malcolm S. Salter, also a professor at Harvard University, but at Harvard Business School, looked at the role of corporations' use of legal means to subvert the intentions underlying the rules of society to gain advantages over competitors, maximise profits, etc. (Salter, 2010, 2019). It is, according to Salter, one of the most corrosive forms of institutional corruption in the business world. The expression that Salter uses for this type of practices is "the gaming of society's rules by corporations". Tax evasion and certain lobbying practices undoubtedly fit this type of manipulation.

An even more radical example of this type of behaviour is, for example, the sort of contest created by Amazon, in 2017, after having decided to establish a second headquarters in North America (which it called HQ2). The company submitted a request for proposals to obtain the most favourable conditions possible for the establishment of HQ2, having received 238 applications from cities in the USA, Canada, and Mexico. Thus, several cities in these countries were put into competition to obtain the "privilege" of hosting HQ2. Another example of institutional corruption, even more radical than the previous one (if that is possible), was the attempt to create a currency, the libra, by a large multinational company, Facebook. Regarding this currency, Stiglitz (2020, p. 16) considers that it should not be allowed and suggests that it is a "vehicle for nurturing illicit activities and laundering the proceeds", that is, the main reason for wanting an alternative currency would be greater ease in participating in activities such as corruption or tax evasion.

7.3 Concluding Comments

I am convinced that to address corruption, tax avoidance and all the other corporate practices occurring at the interface between politics and business, one needs CSR instruments that deal with them in an integrated fashion. To adequately deal with corporate corruption, one has to also address tax and lobbying issues, among others. Regarding tax behaviour, the case is similar, given that one has to address issues pertaining to corporate lobbying. In this perspective, I consider the recent Transparency International UK's "Principles and guidance for anti-corruption corporate transparency" (Transparency International UK, 2020), which namely address the reporting of several aspects (beneficial ownership, organisational structure, corporate political engagement, and tax-related issues on a country-by-country basic), a very interesting development. I believe that used in combination with the relevant GRI Standards, it can offer corporations and all those interested in these issues the basis for the development of a framework to integratively address these issues. But this would be the topic of another book.

References

Amit, E., Koralnik, J., Posten, A. C., Muethel, M., & Lessig, L. (2017). Institutional corruption revisited: Exploring open questions within the institutional corruption literature. *Southern California Interdisciplinary Law Journal, 26*, 447–467.

Brulle, R. J. (2018). The climate lobby: a sectoral analysis of lobbying spending on climate change in the USA, 2000 to 2016. *Climatic Change, 149*(3), 289–303.

Carbon Market Watch. (2020). Never wasting a crisis: Industry climate lobbying during the covid-19 pandemic exposed. *Carbon Market Watch Briefing*. Accessed February 4, 2021, from https://carbonmarketwatch.org/wp-content/uploads/2020/05/Never-wasting-a-crisis-1.pdf

Cobham, A., Janský, P., & Meinzer, M. (2018). A half-century of resistance to corporate disclosure. *Transnational Corporations, 25*(3), 1–27.

Cory, J., Lerner, M., & Osgood, I. (2021). Supply chain linkages and the extended carbon coalition. *American Journal of Political Science, 65*(1), 69–87.

Dialer, D., & Richter, M. (Eds.). (2019). *Lobbying in the European Union: Strategies, dynamics and trends*. Springer.

Fair Tax Mark. (2019). *The Silicon Six and their $100 billion global tax gap*. Fair tax Mark.

Fisher, M. (2013). The anti-Americanism of Jackie Chan. *The Washington Post*. Accessed February 4, 2021, from https://www.washingtonpost.com/news/worldviews/wp/2013/01/10/the-anti-americanism-of-jackie-chan/

Fleming, P., & Zyglidopoulos, S. C. (2009). *Charting corporate corruption: Agency, structure and escalation*. Edward Elgar.

Grasso, M. (2019). Oily politics: A critical assessment of the oil and gas industry's contribution to climate change. *Energy Research & Social Science, 50*, 106–115.

Graycar, A., & Monaghan, O. (2015). Rich country corruption. *International Journal of Public Administration, 38*(8), 586–595.

Lessig, L. (2013). "Institutional corruption" defined. *The Journal of Law, Medicine & Ethics, 41*(3), 553–555.

Lessig, L. (2015). Corrupt and unequal, both. *Fordham Law Review, 84*, 445–452.

Meng, K. C., & Rode, A. (2019). The social cost of lobbying over climate policy. *Nature Climate Change, 9*(6), 472–476.

Mintzberg, H. (2016). *Which country is more corrupt: Brazil or the United States?* Accessed February 4, 2021, from https://mintzberg.org/blog/Brazil-corruption

OECD. (2016). *Financing Democracy: Funding of political parties and election campaigns and the risk of policy capture*. OECD.

Oluwole, F. (2019). Getting past the lobby! The alliance for lobbying transparency and ethics regulation (ALTER-EU). In D. Dialer & M. Richter (Eds.), *Lobbying in the European Union: Strategies, dynamics and trends* (pp. 291–303). Springer.

Oxfam America. (2017). *Rigged reform: US companies are dodging billions in taxes but proposed reforms will make things worse*. Oxfam America.

Ross, L. (2020). Cashing in on COVID: Tax breaks, royalties and stimulus loans. *Friends of the Earth*.

Sachs, J. D. (2011). *The global economy's corporate crime wave*. Project Syndicate. Accessed February 4, 2021, from https://www.project-syndicate.org/commentary/the-global-economy-s-corporate-crime-wave?barrier=accesspaylog

Sachs, J. D. (2016). *To end corruption, start with the US and UK. They allow it in broad daylight*. Project Syndicate. Accessed February 4, 2021, from https://www.theguardian.com/commentisfree/2016/may/12/anti-corruption-summit-us-united-kingdom-tax-havens

Salter, M. S. (2010). Lawful but corrupt: Gaming and the problem of institutional corruption in the private sector. Harvard Business School Research Paper No. 11-060.

Salter, M. S. (2019). *Rehabilitating corporate purpose*. Harvard Business School NOM Unit Working Paper No. 19-104.

Silva, M. (2019). The European Union's revolving door problem. In D. Dialer & M. Richter (Eds.), *Lobbying in the European Union: Strategies, dynamics and trends* (pp. 273–289). Springer.

Stiglitz, J. E. (2020). Key challenges facing modern finance: Making the financial sector serve society. *Finance: Theory and Practice, 24*(2), 6–21.

Transparency International UK. (2020). *Open business: Principles and guidance for anti-corruption corporate transparency*. Transparency International UK.

UNGC. (2013). *A guide for Anti-corruption risk assessment*. UNGC.

Wilkinson, P. (2015). *Wise counsel or dark arts? Principles and guidance for responsible corporate political engagement*. Transparency International UK.